FOR ORGANS, PIANOS & ELECTRONIC KEYBOARDS

127

JOHN DENVER'S GREATEST HITS

T0042525

E-Z Play TODAY chord notation is designed for playing **standard chord positions** or **single key chords** on all **major brand organs** and **portable keyboards.**

Contents

ISBN 978-0-7935-3175-2

cherry lane
music company

EXCLUSIVELY DISTRIBUTED BY
HAL•LEONARD
CORPORATION
7777 W. BLUEMOUND RD. P.O. BOX 13819 MILWAUKEE, WI 53213

Annie's Song

Registration 1
Rhythm: Waltz

Words and Music by
John Denver

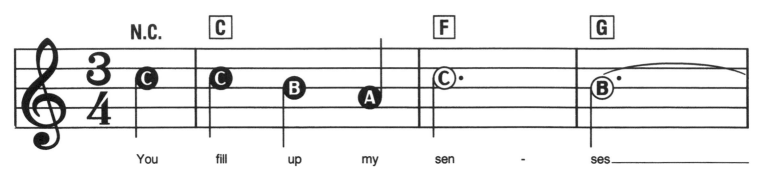

You fill up my sen - ses

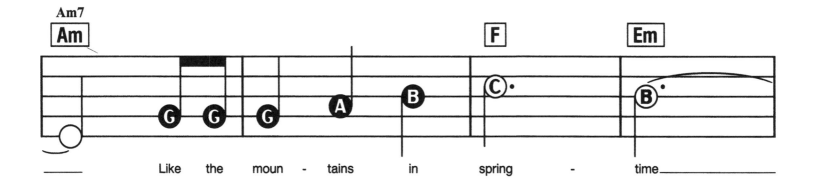

like a night in a for - est,

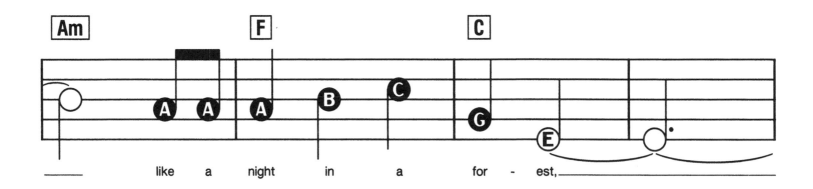

Like the moun - tains in spring - time

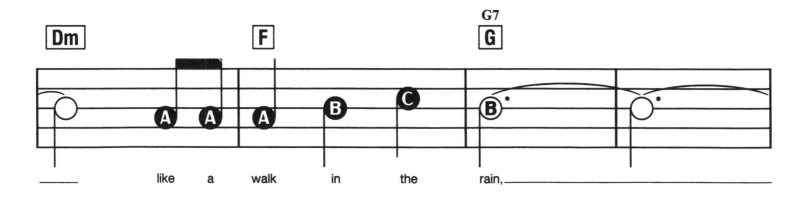

like a walk in the rain,

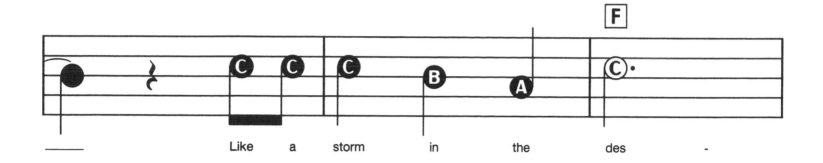

Like a storm in the des -

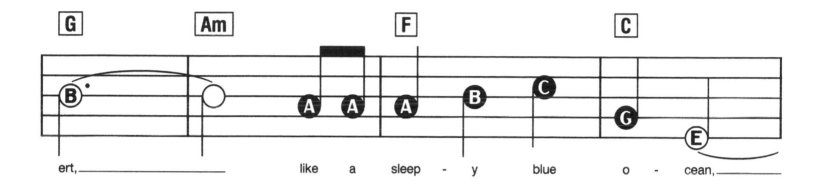

ert,_____ like a sleep - y blue o - cean,_____

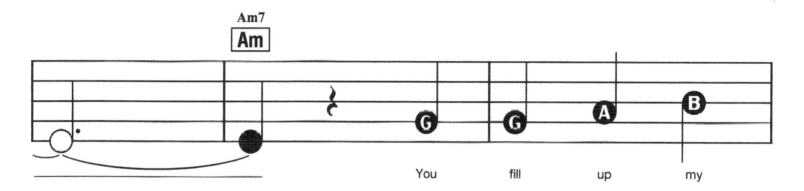

You fill up my

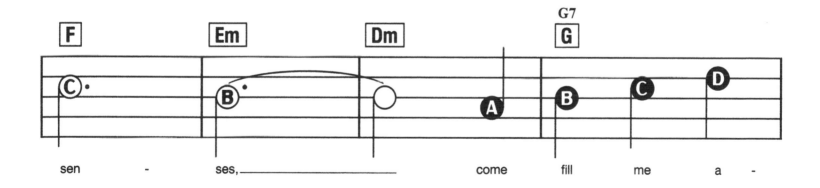

sen - ses,_____ come fill me a -

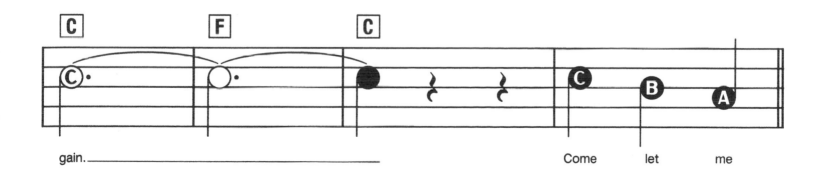

gain._____ Come let me

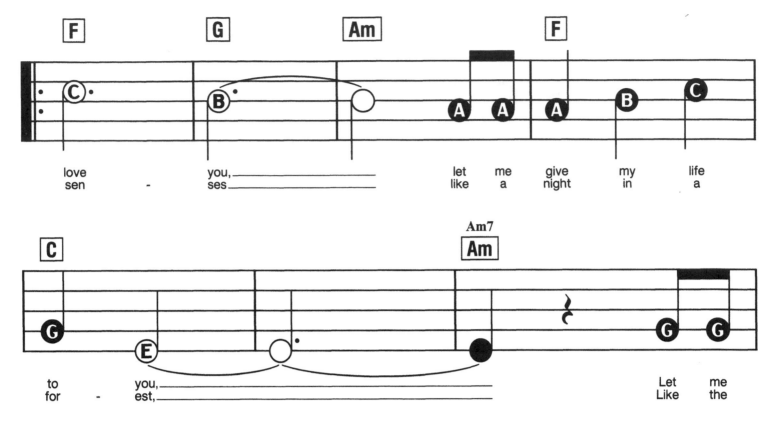

love | you, | | let | me | give | my | life
sen - | ses | | like | a | night | in | a

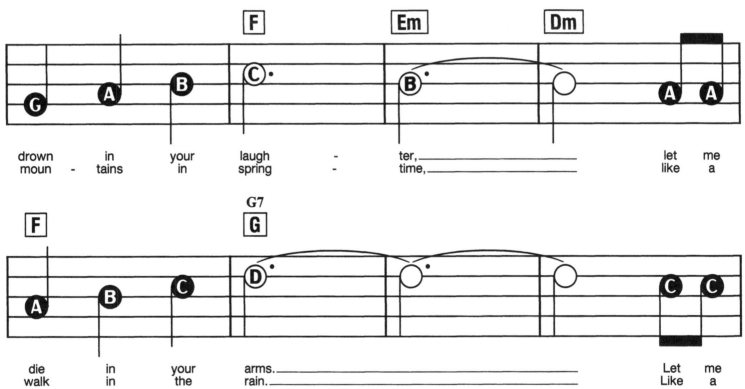

to | you, | | | Let | me
for - | est, | | | Like | the

drown | in | your | laugh | - | ter, | | let | me
moun - | tains | in | spring | - | time, | | like | a

die | in | your | arms. | | Let | me
walk | in | the | rain. | | Like | a

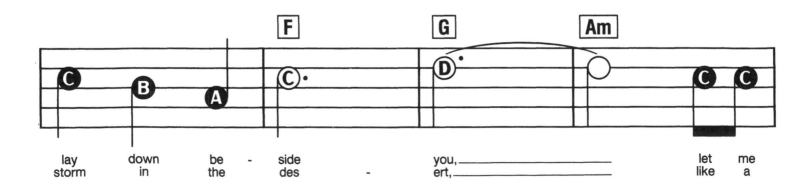

lay | down | be - | side | you, | | let | me
storm | in | the | des | - | ert, | | like | a

5

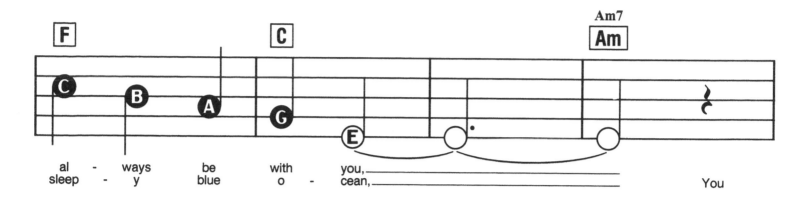

al - ways be with you,_____ You
sleep - y blue o - cean,_____

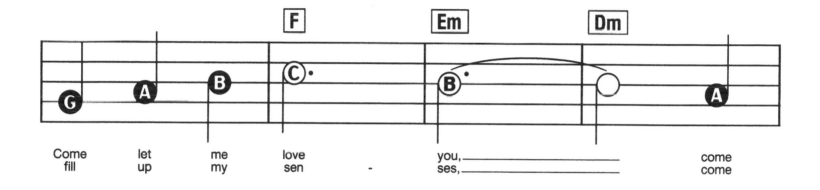

Come let me love you,_____ come
fill up my sen - ses,_____ come

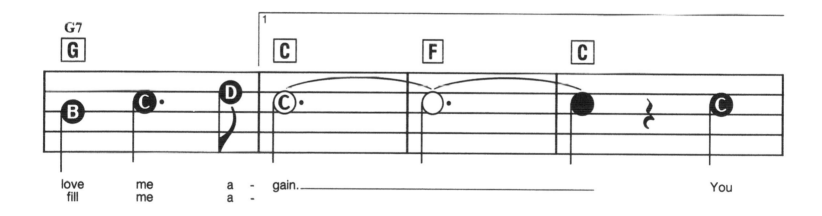

love me a - gain._____ You
fill me a -

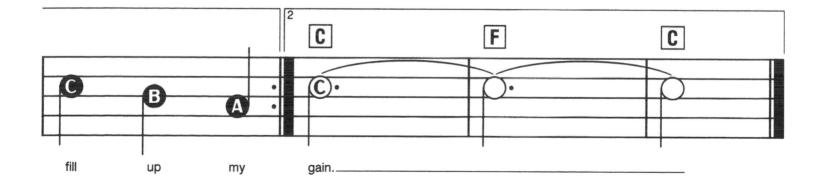

fill up my gain._____

Autograph

Registration 4
Rhythm: Rock

Words and Music by
John Denver

Here I am, and clos - ing my eyes a - gain,
Then I go and o - pen my eyes a - gain,
Say a pray'r and o - pen your heart a - gain,

Try - ing so hard not to see all the things that I
Love in your eyes is the thing all that I'd most like to
You are the love and the light that we all need to

see. Al - most will - ing to lie a - gain,
see. I'd be will - ing to die a - gain,
see. Al - ways will - ing to shine and then

I
To

swear that it just is - n't so, It just is - n't
know of a place and a time where it al - ways could
Peace on this earth is the way that it al - ways can

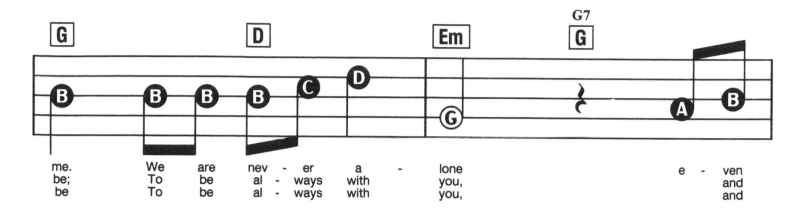

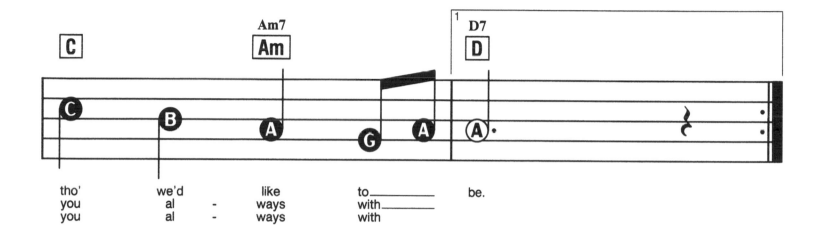

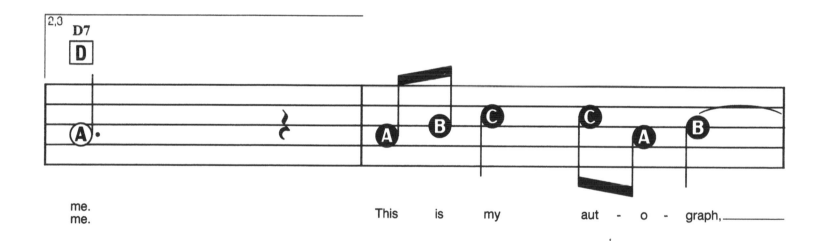

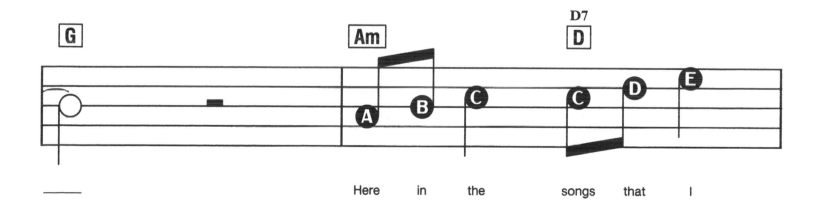

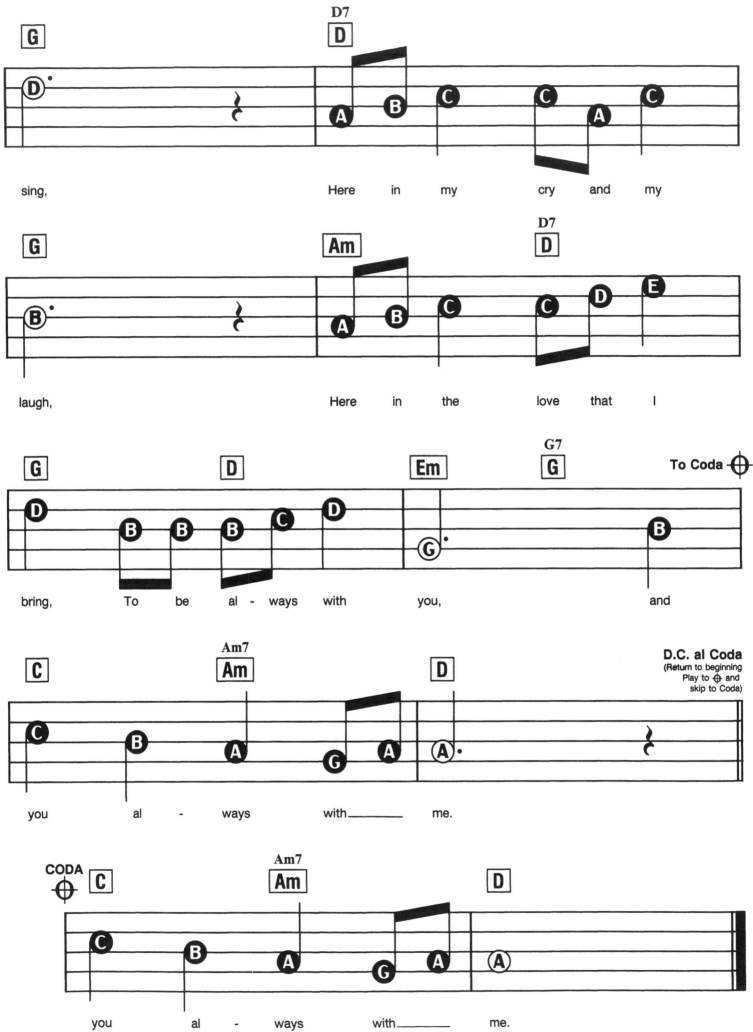

Back Home Again

Registration 7
Rhythm: Country

Words and Music by
John Denver

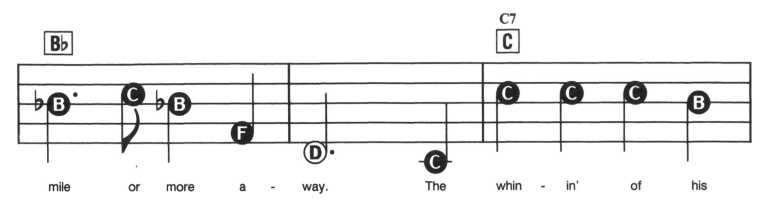

mile or more a - way. The whin - in' of his

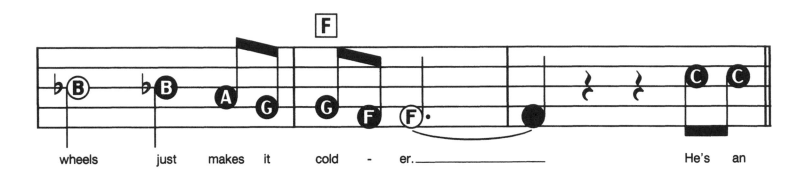

wheels just makes it cold - er.____ He's an

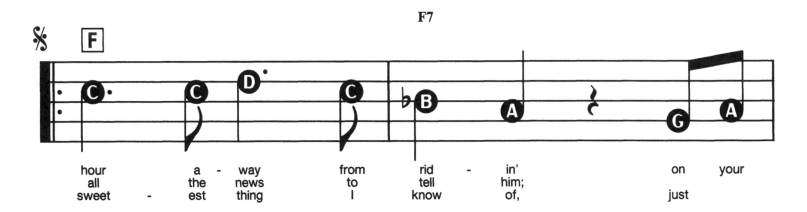

hour   a - way   from   rid - in'   on   your
all   the   news   to   tell   him;   just
sweet - est   thing   I   know   of,

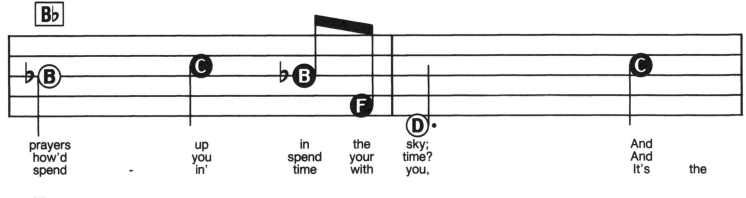

prayers   up   in   the   sky;   And
how'd   you   spend   your   time?   And
spend - in'   time   with   you,   It's   the

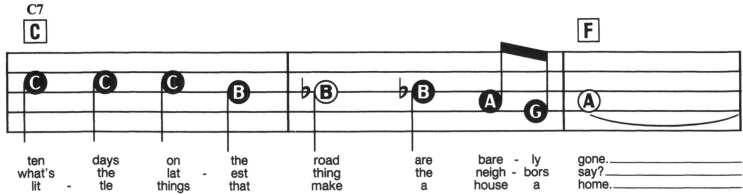

ten   days   on   the   road   are   bare - ly   gone.____
what's   the   lat - est   thing   the   neigh - bors   say?____
lit - tle   things   that   make   a   house   a   home.____

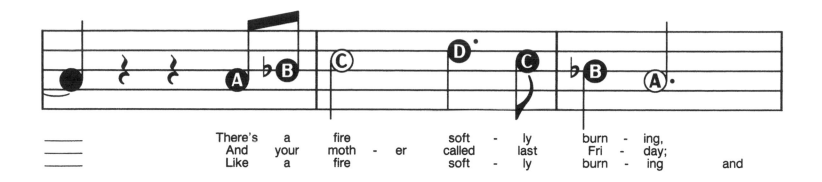

F7

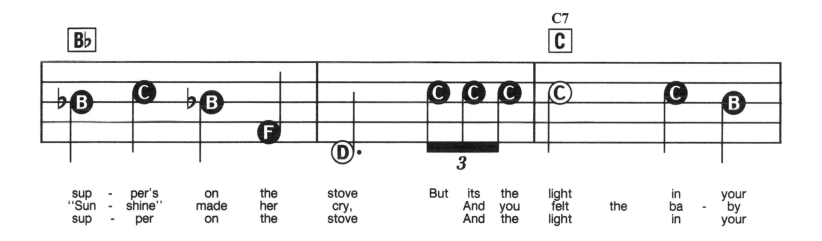

There's a fire soft - ly burn - ing,
And your moth - er called last Fri - day;
Like a fire soft - ly burn - ing and

Bb   C7
C

sup - per's on the stove But its the light in your
"Sun - shine" made her cry, And you felt the ba - by
sup - per on the stove And the light in your

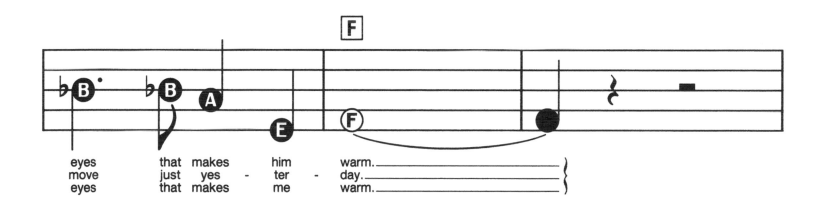

F

eyes that makes him warm.
move just yes - ter - day.
eyes that makes me warm.

Chorus

Bb   C7
C

Hey, it's good to be back home a -

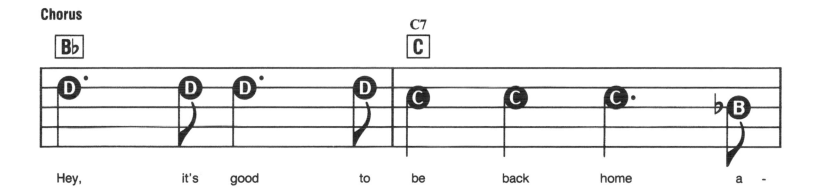

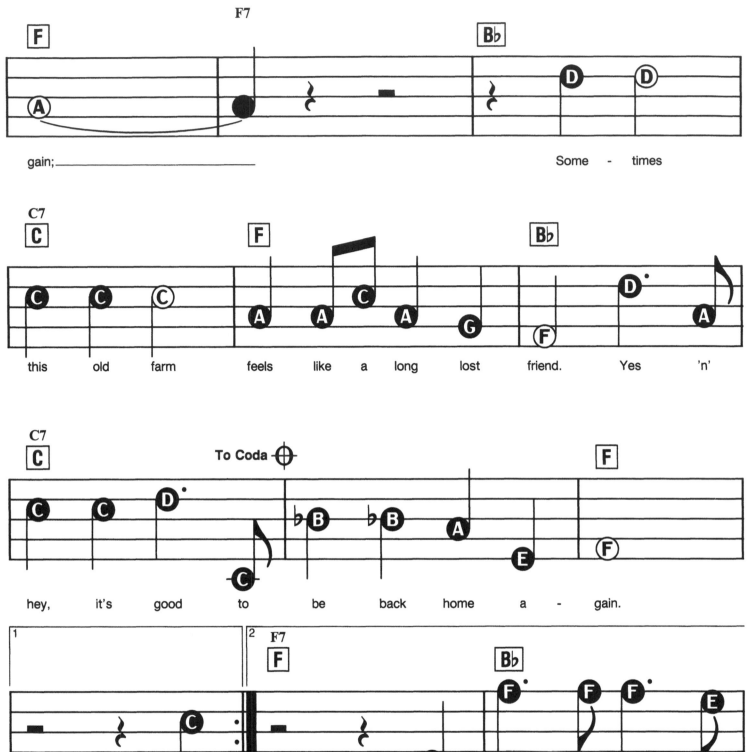

gain;   Some - times this old farm feels like a long lost friend. Yes 'n'

hey, it's good to be back home a - gain.

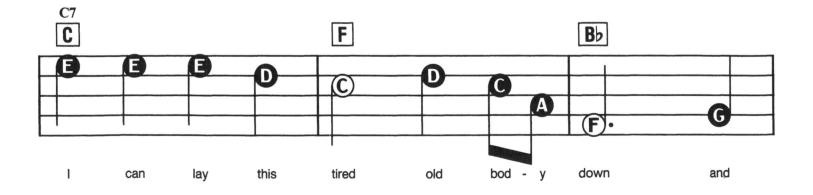

There's   And oh, the time that I can lay this tired old bod - y down and

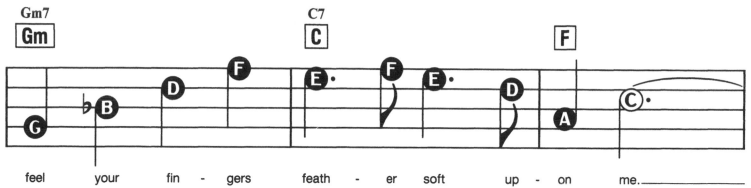

feel your fin - gers feath - er soft up - on me.

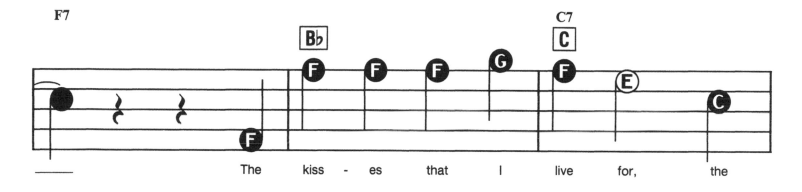

The kiss - es that I live for, the

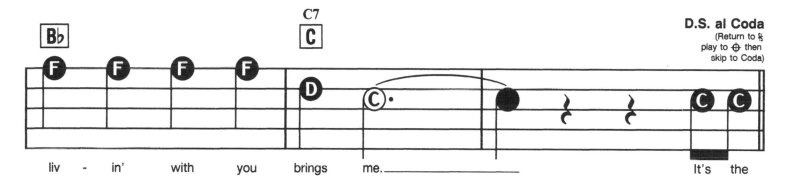

love that lights my way, The hap - pi - ness that

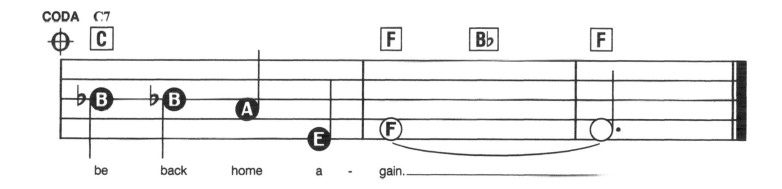

liv - in' with you brings me. It's the

D.S. al Coda
(Return to 𝄋
play to ⊕ then
skip to Coda)

CODA

be back home a - gain.

A Baby Just Like You

Registration 4
Rhythm: Ballad

Words and Music by
John Denver and Joe Henry

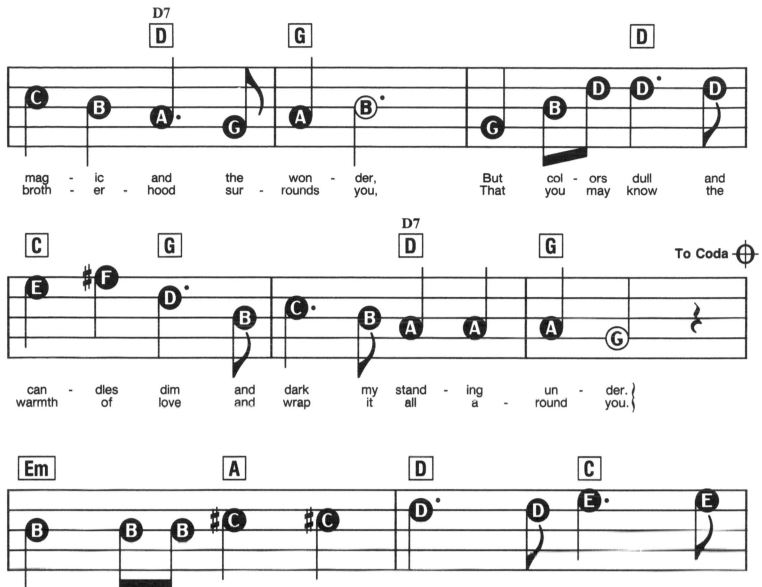

mag - ic and the won - der, But col - ors dull and
broth - er - hood sur - rounds you, That you may know and the

can - dles dim and dark my stand - ing un - der.
warmth of love and wrap it all a - round you.

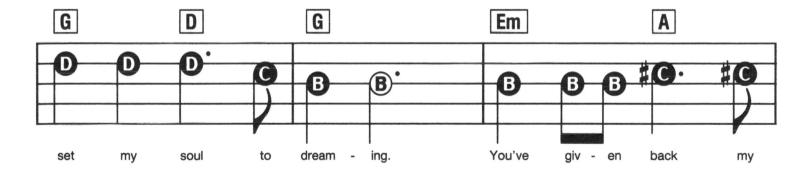

Oh, lit - tle an - gel, shin - ing light, you've

set my soul to dream - ing. You've giv - en back my

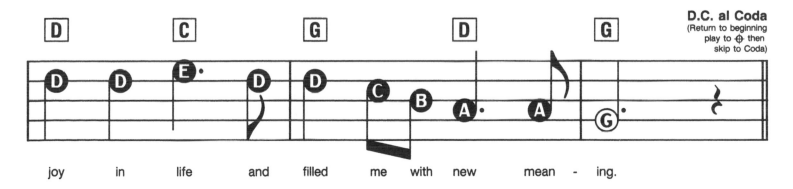

D.C. al Coda
(Return to beginning
play to ⊕ then
skip to Coda)

joy in life and filled me with new mean - ing.

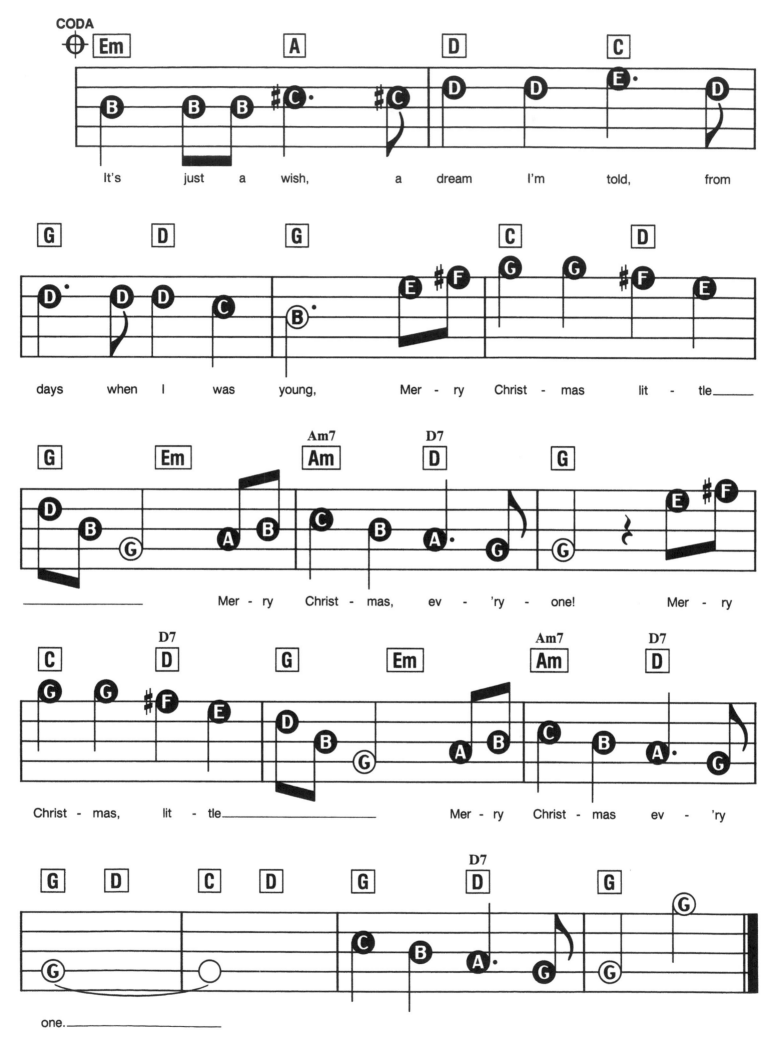

Follow Me

Registration 7
Rhythm: Country

Words and Music by
John Denver

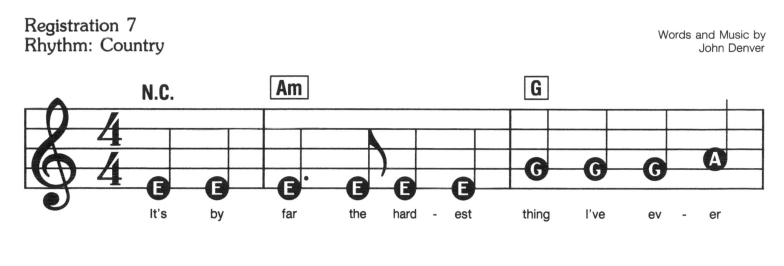

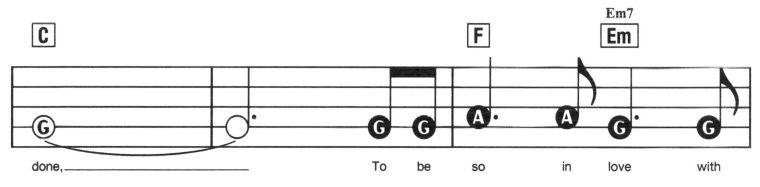

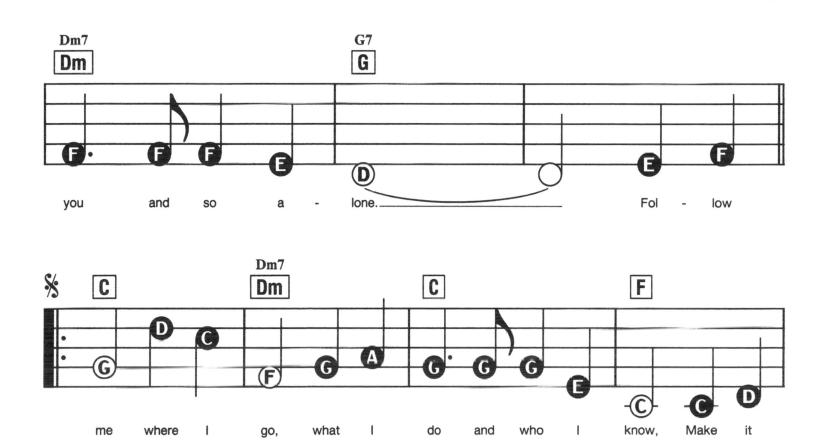

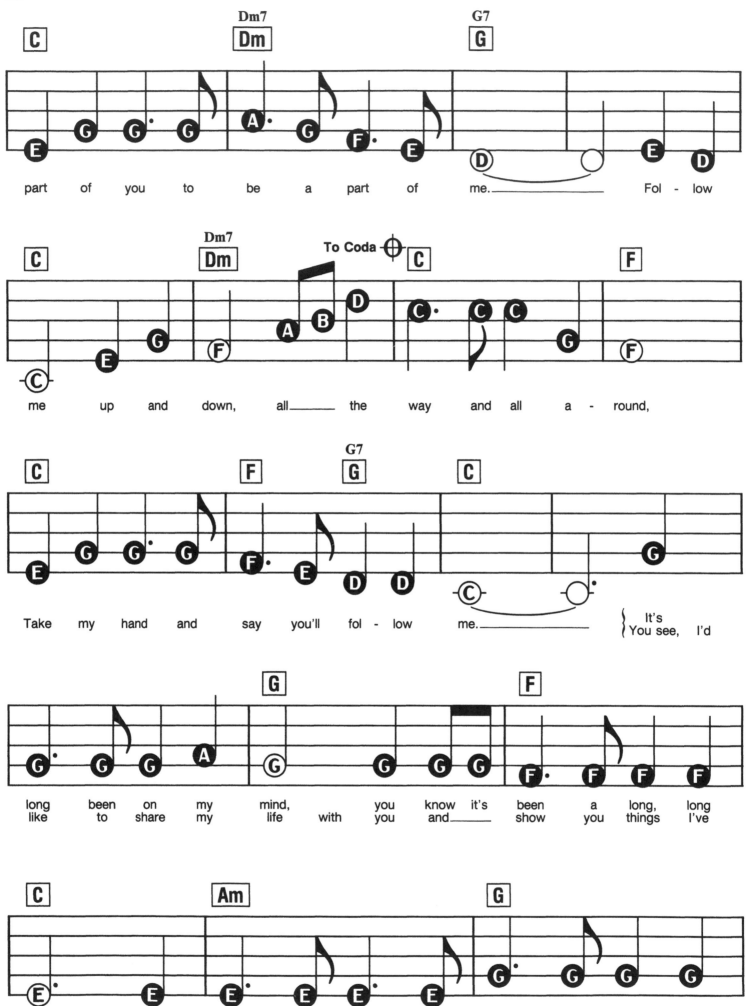

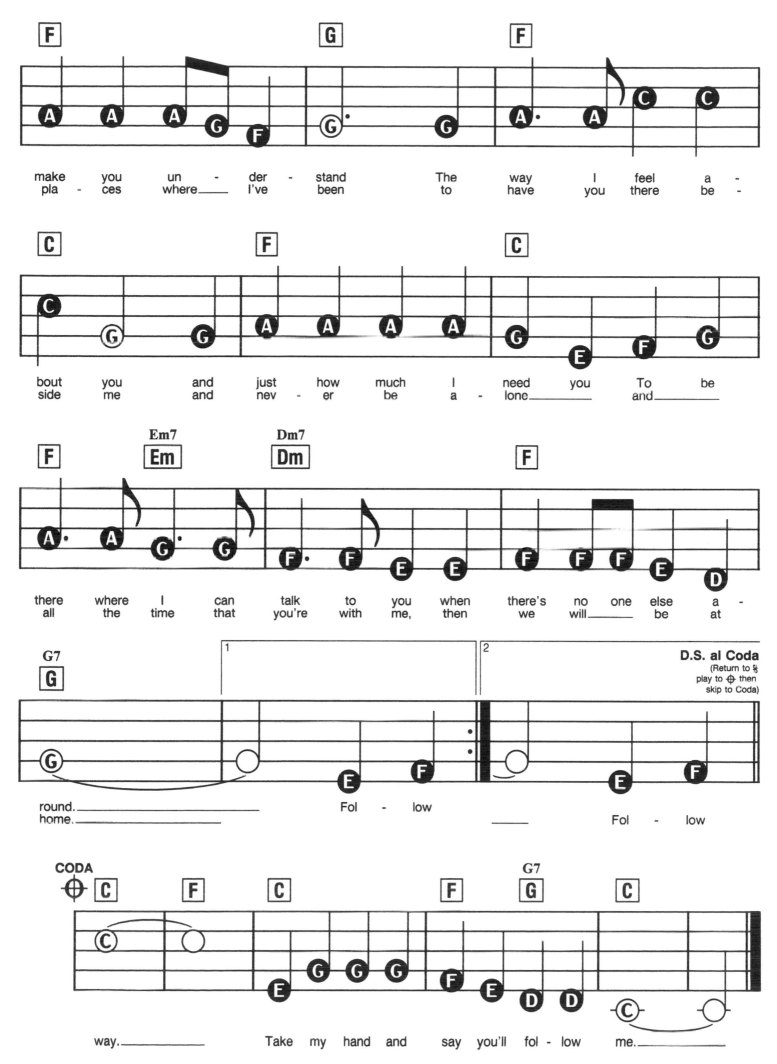

Calypso

Registration 4
Rhythm: Waltz

Words and Music by
John Denver

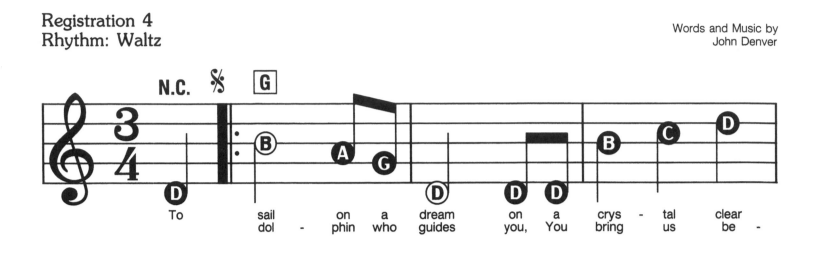

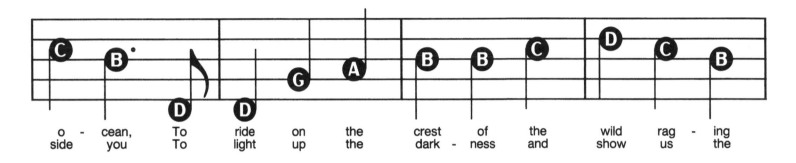

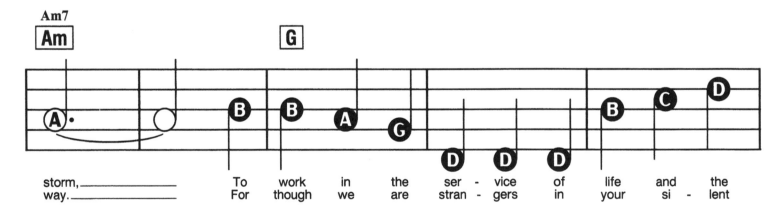

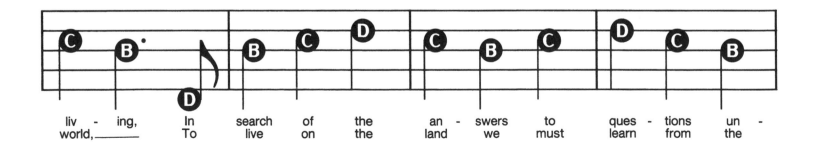

21

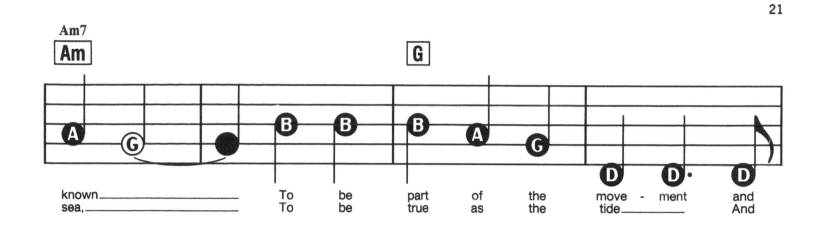

known To be part of the move - ment and
sea, To be true as the tide And

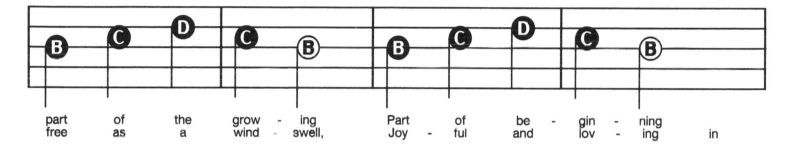

part of the grow - ing Part of be - gin - ning
free as a wind - swell, Joy - ful and lov - ing in

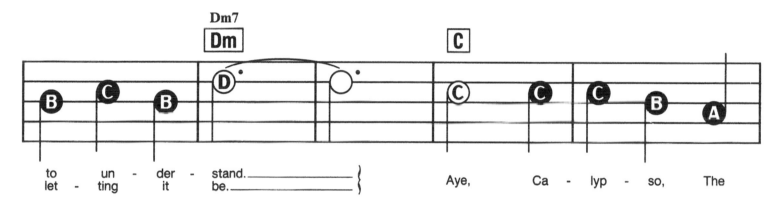

to un - der - stand. Aye, Ca - lyp - so, The
let - ting it be.

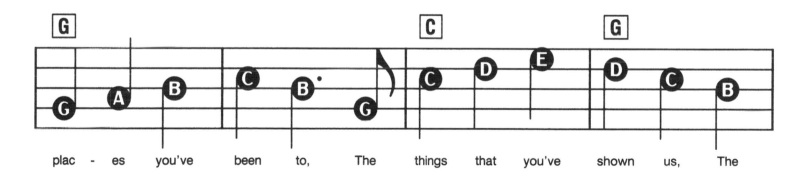

plac - es you've been to, The things that you've shown us, The

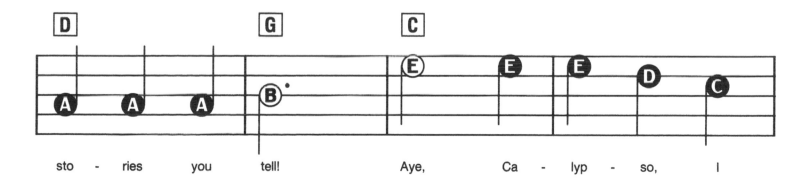

sto - ries you tell! Aye, Ca - lyp - so, I

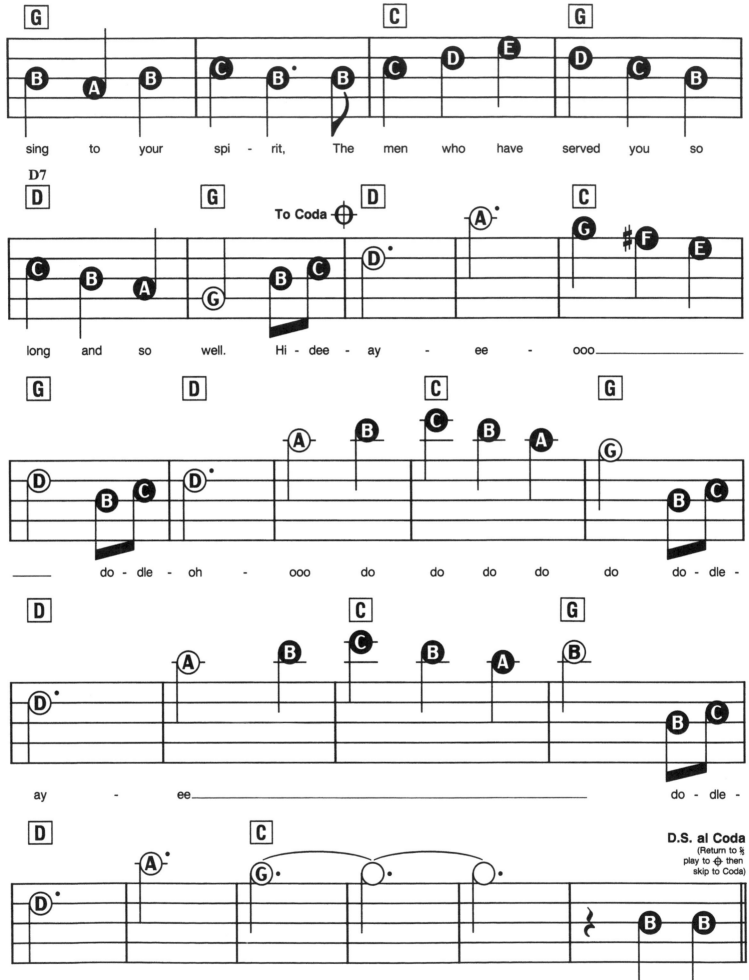

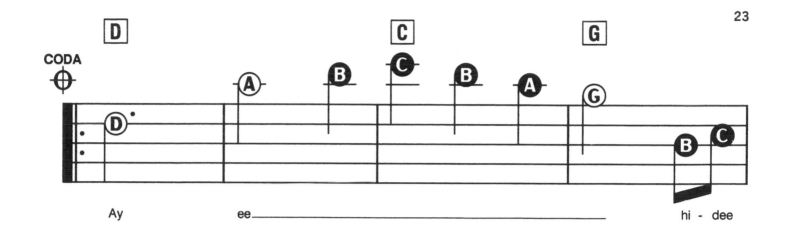

Ay   ee_____ hi - dee

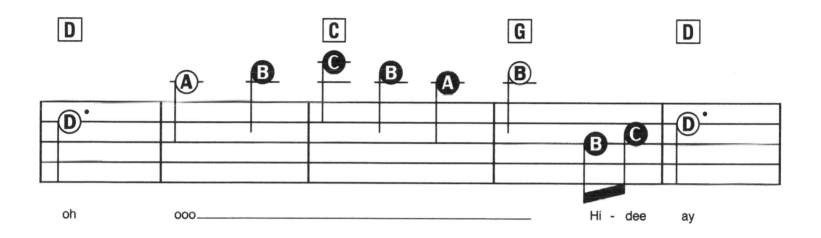

oh   ooo_____ Hi - dee   ay

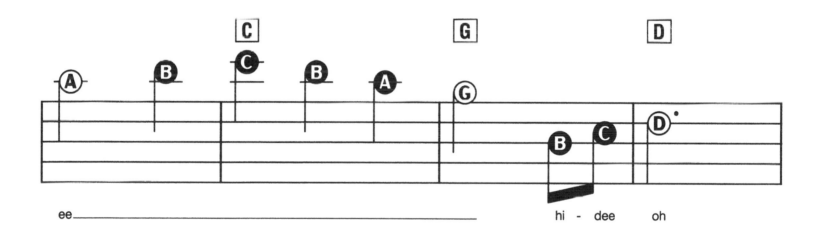

ee_____ hi - dee   oh

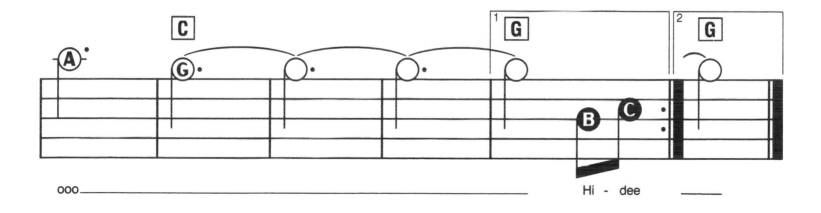

ooo_____ Hi - dee _____

Fly Away

Registration 7
Rhythm: Fox Trot or Ballad

Words and Music by
John Denver

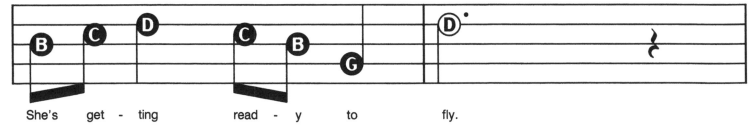

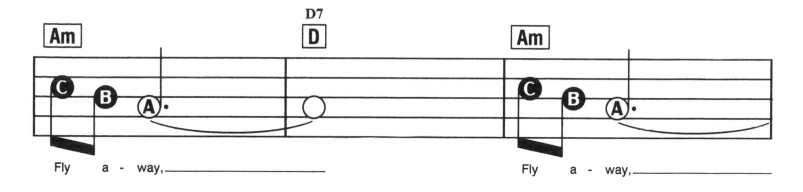

Fly a - way,

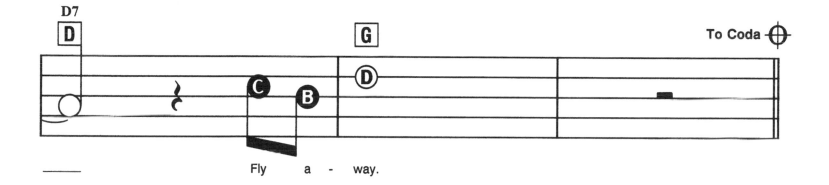

Fly a - way.

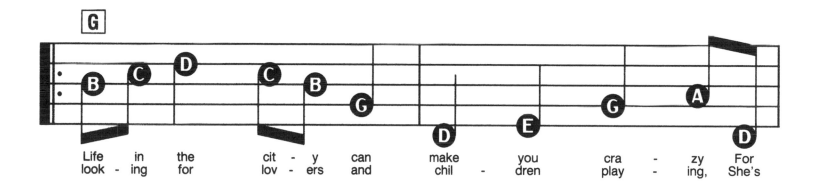

Life in the cit - y can make you cra - zy, For
look - ing the for lov - ers and chil - dren play - ing, She's

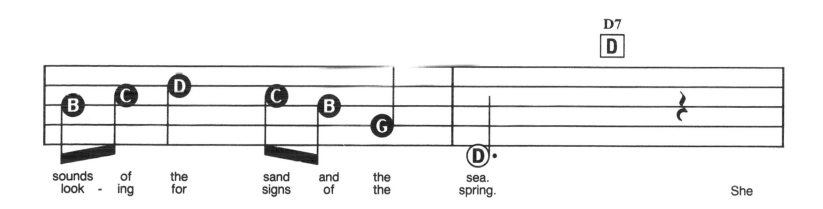

sounds of the sand and the sea.
look - ing for signs of the spring.

She

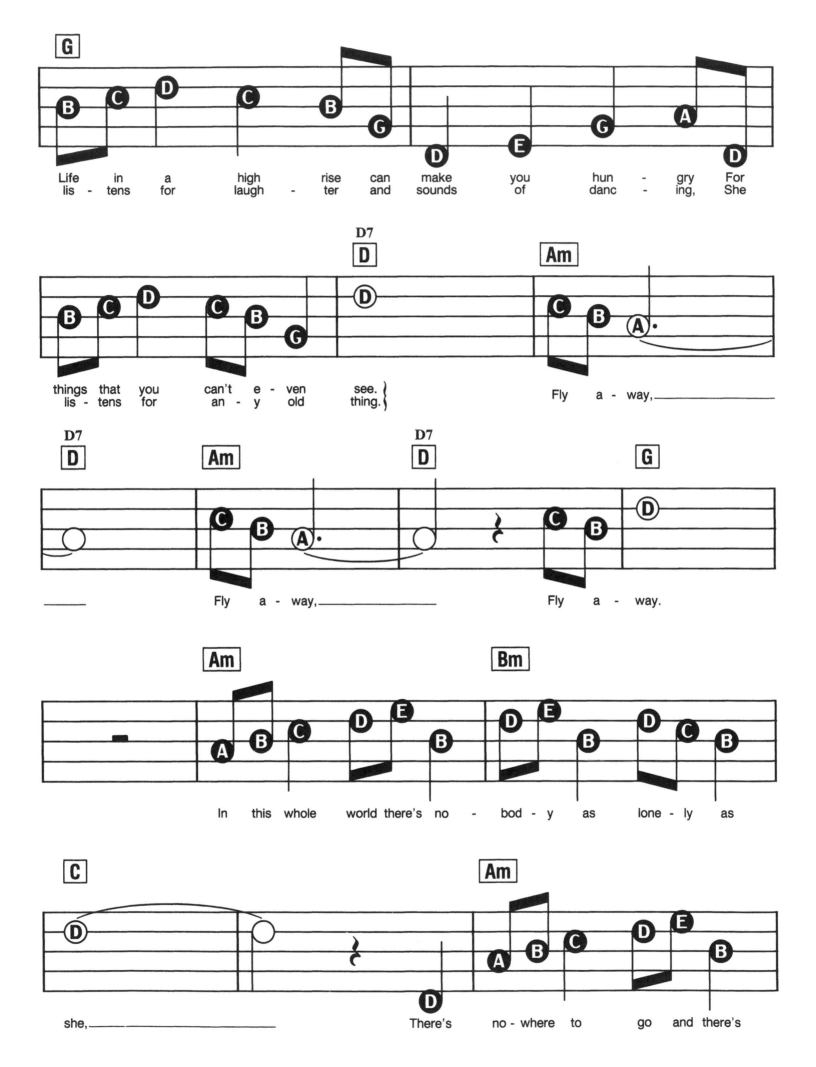

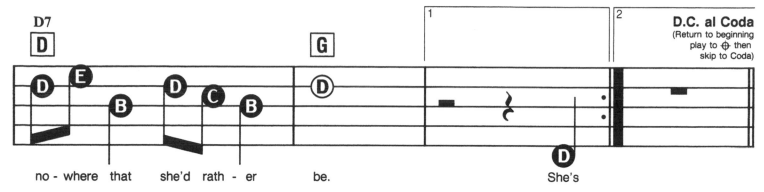

no - where that she'd rath - er be. She's

D.C. al Coda
(Return to beginning
play to ⊕ then
skip to Coda)

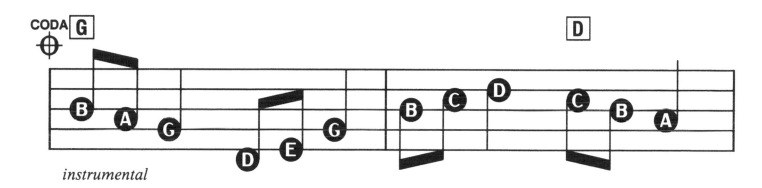

instrumental

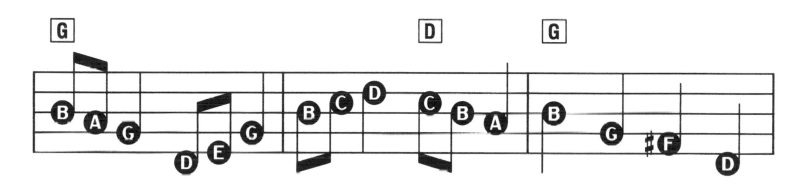

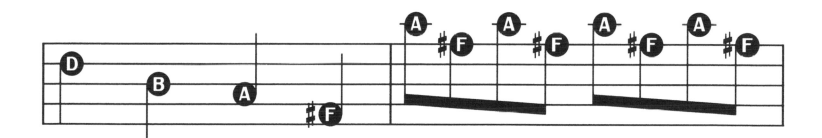

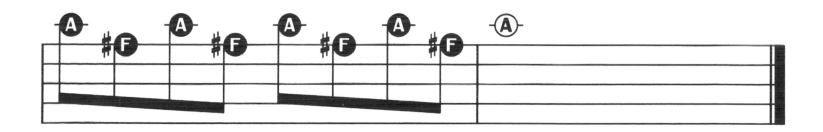

For Baby (For Bobbie)

Registration 1
Rhythm: Fox Trot or Ballad

Words and Music by
John Denver

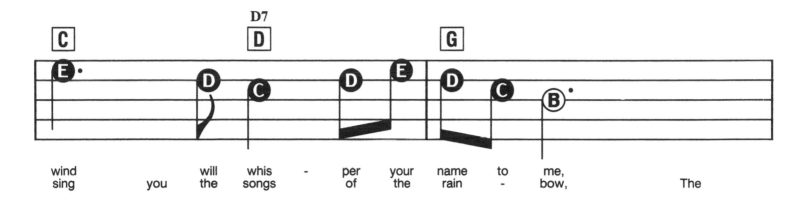

wind / sing
you
will / the
whis / songs
per / of
your / the
name / rain
to / bow,
me,
The

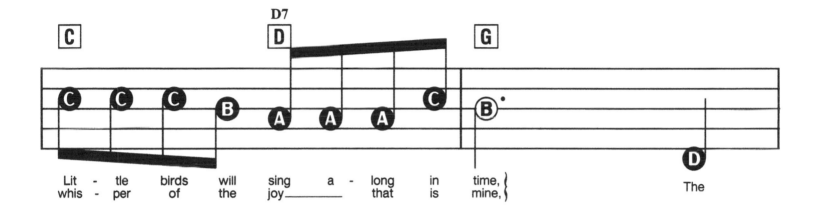

Lit / whis
tle / per
birds / of
will / the
sing / joy
a / long
in / that
time, / is
mine,
The

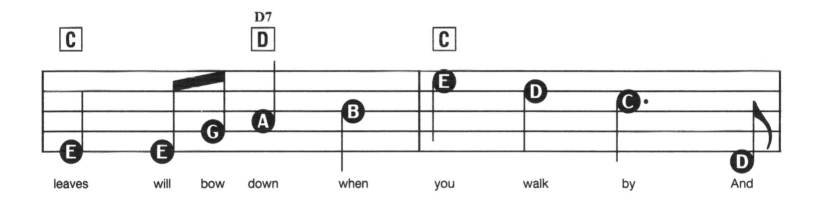

leaves
will
bow
down
when
you
walk
by
And

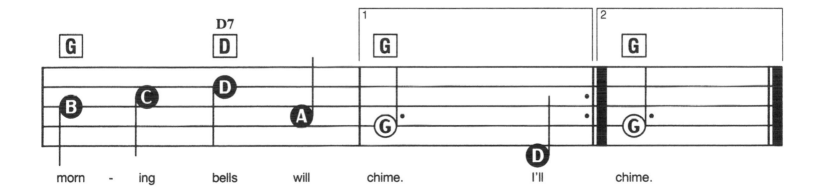

morn
ing
bells
will
chime.
I'll
chime.

Friends With You

Registration 1
Rhythm: Fox Trot or Ballad

Words and Music by
Bill Danoff and Taffy Nivert

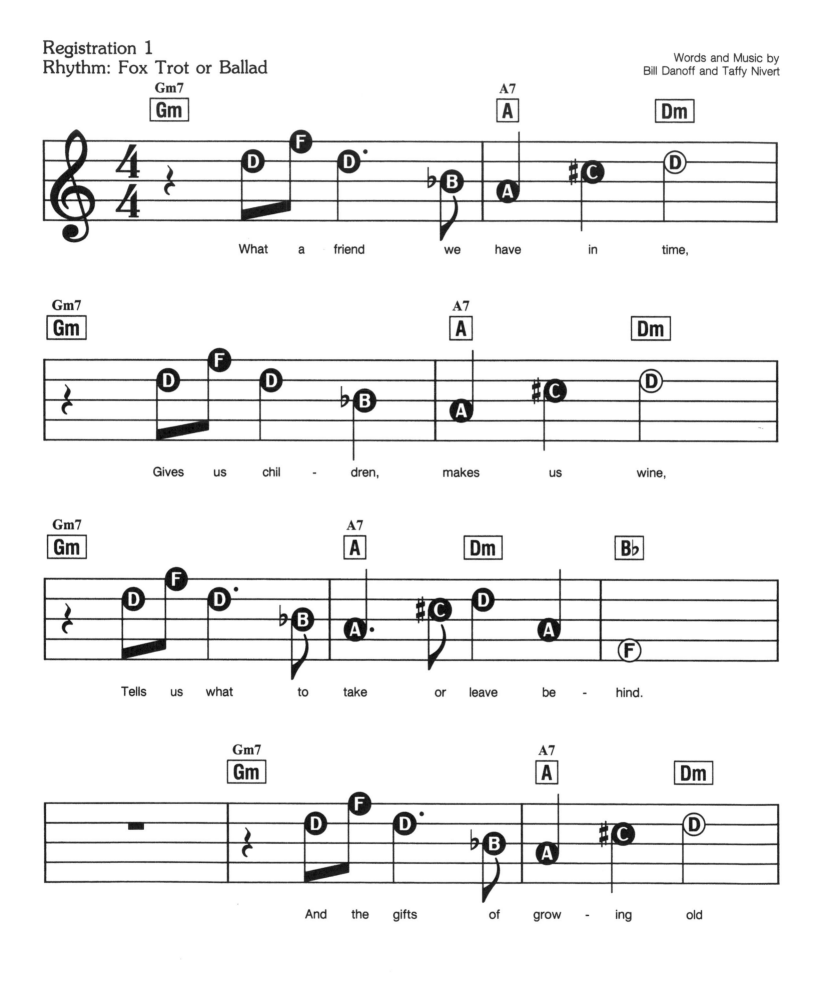

31

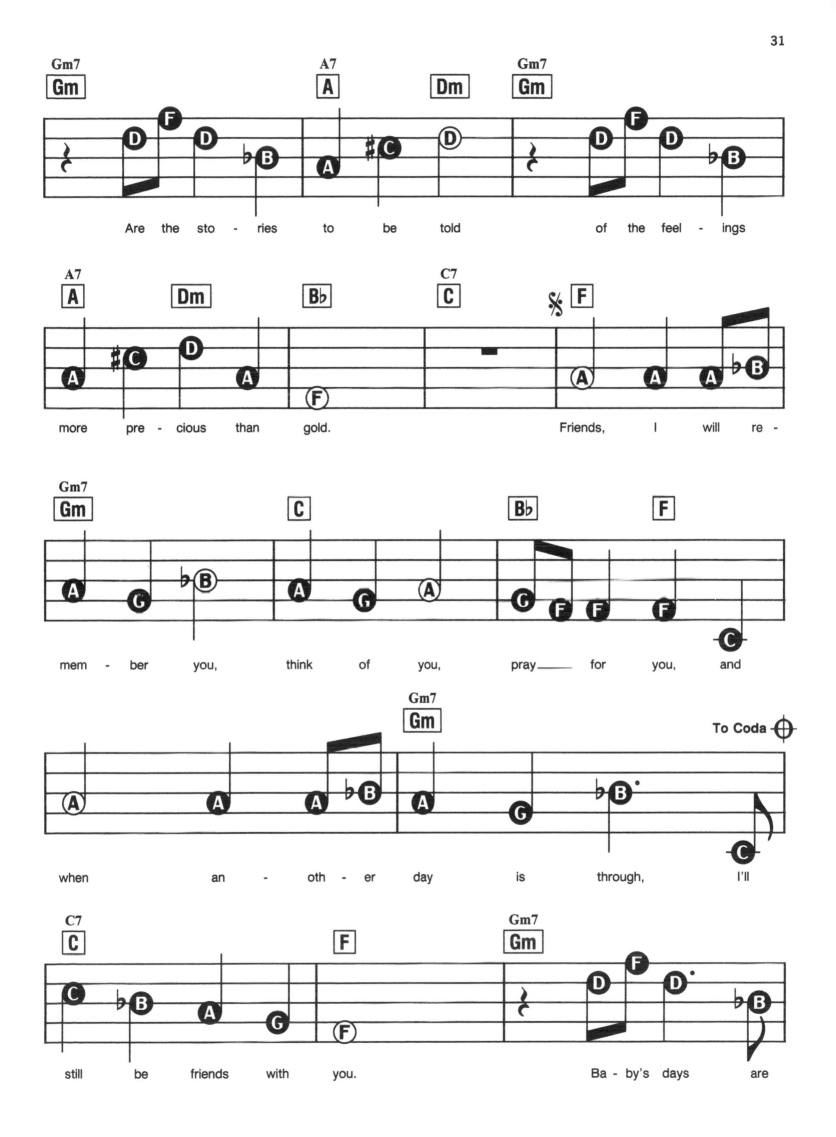

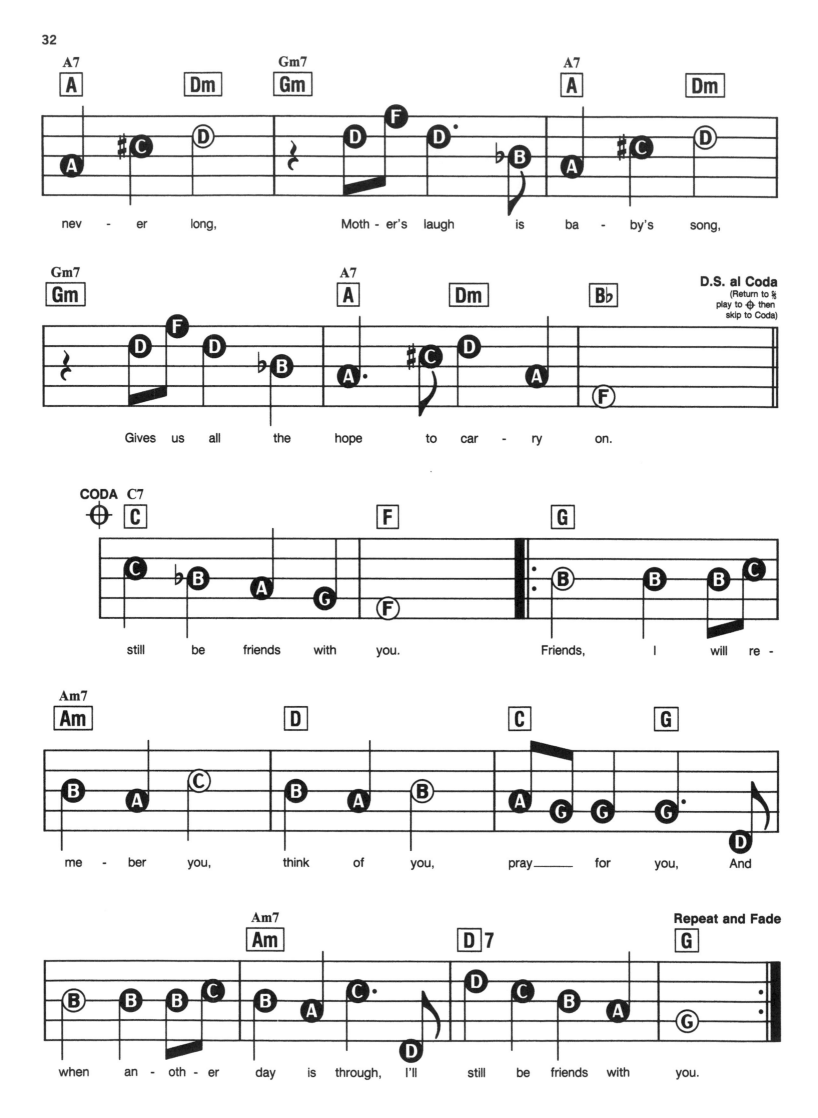

Garden Song

Registration 4
Rhythm: Country

Words and Music by
David B. Mallett

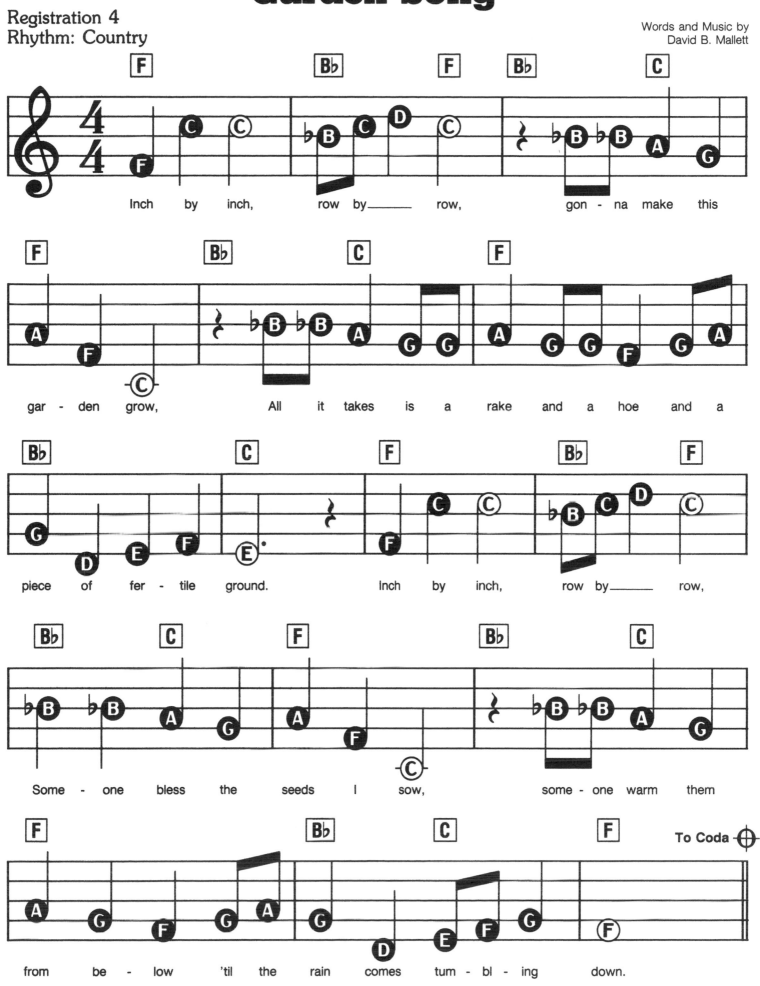

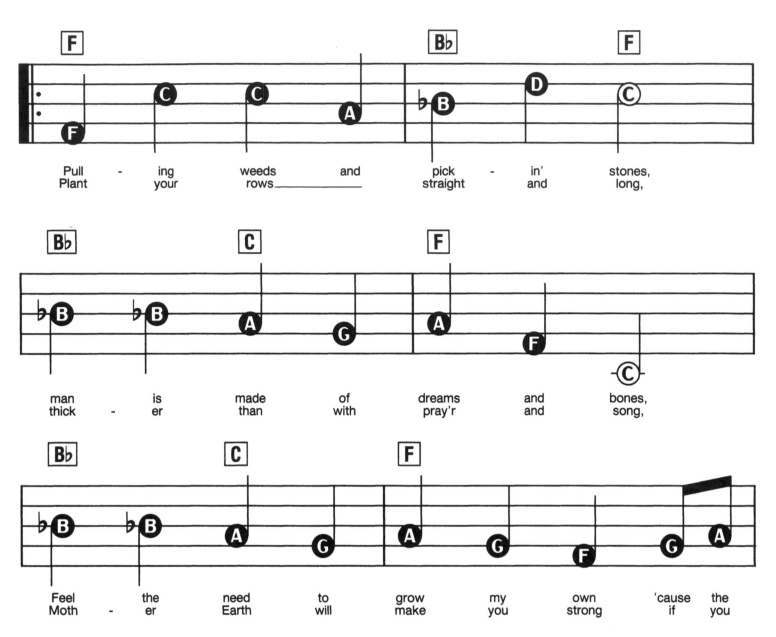

Pull - ing weeds and pick - in' stones,
Plant your rows_____ straight and long,

man - is made of dreams and bones,
thick - er than with pray'r and song,

Feel the need to grow my own 'cause the
Moth - er Earth will make you strong if you

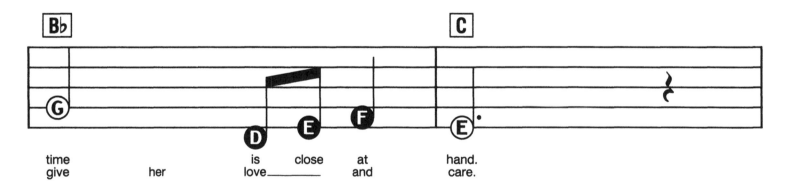

time is close at hand.
give her love_____ and care.

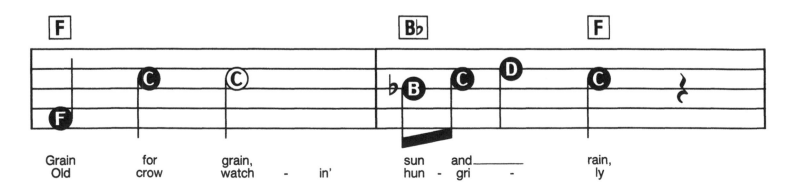

Grain for grain, watch - in' sun and_____ rain,
Old crow grain, hun - gri - ly

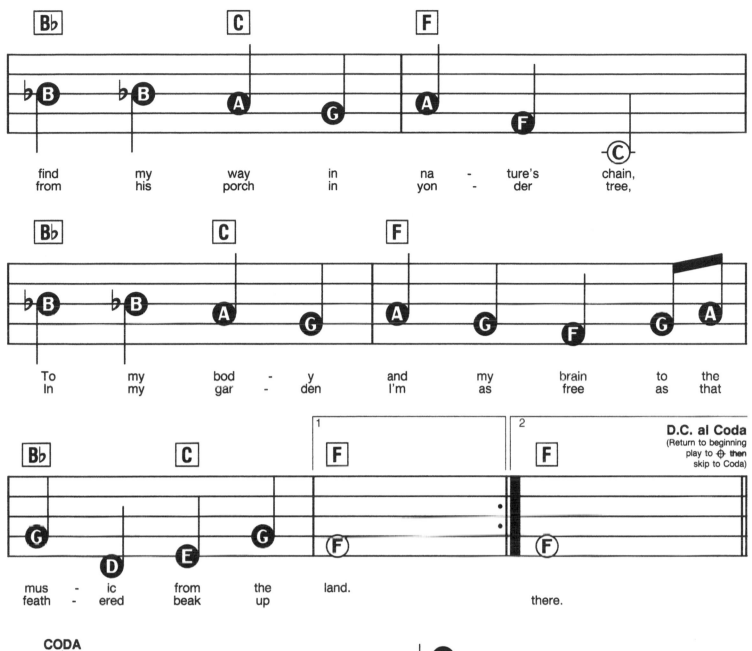

find my way in na - ture's chain,
from his porch in yon - der tree,

To my bod - y and my brain to the
In my gar - den I'm as free as that

mus - ic from the land.
feath - ered beak up there.

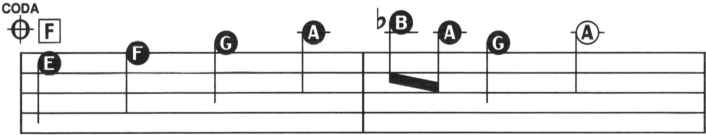

CODA

instrumental

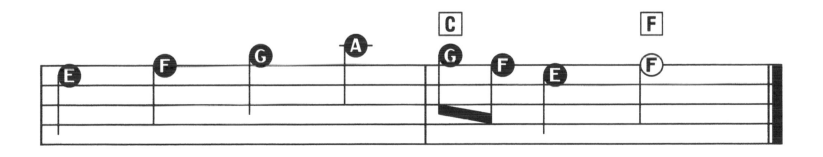

I Want To Live

Registration 1
Rhythm: Fox Trot or Ballad

Words and Music by
John Denver

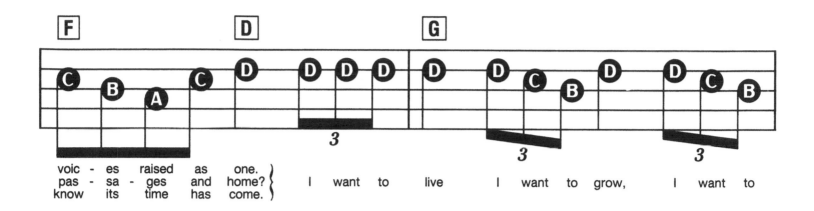

voic - es raised as one.
pas - sa - ges and home?
know its time has come. I want to live I want to grow, I want to

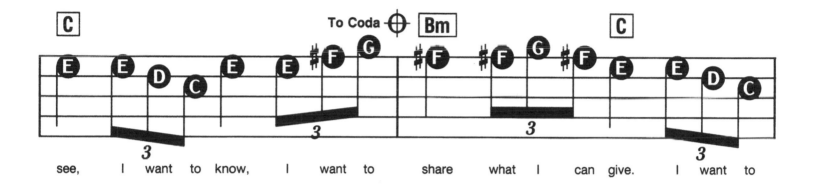

see, I want to know, I want to share what I can give. I want to

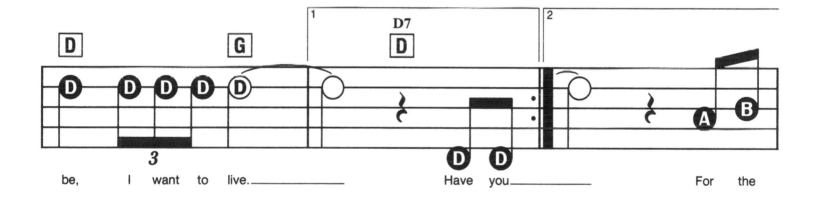

be, I want to live. Have you For the

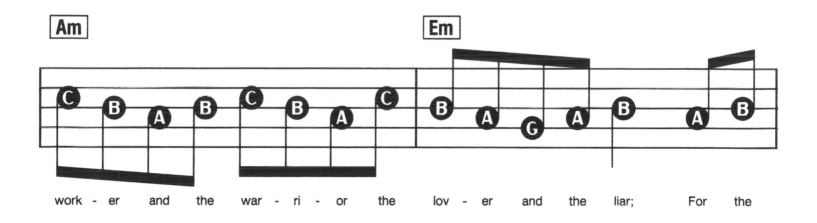

work - er and the war - ri - or the lov - er and the liar; For the

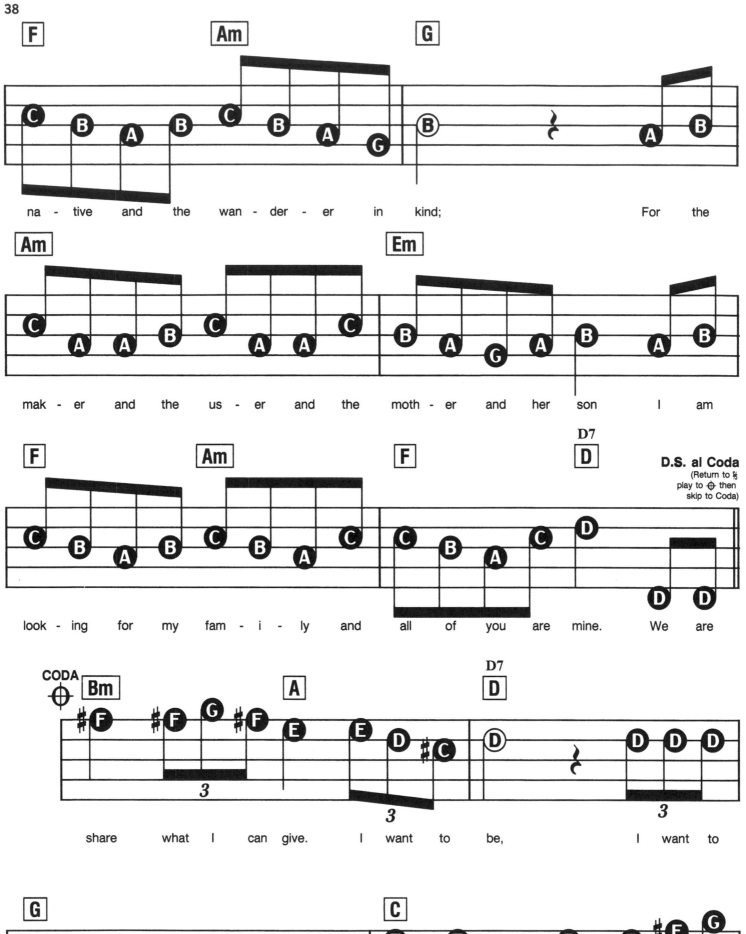

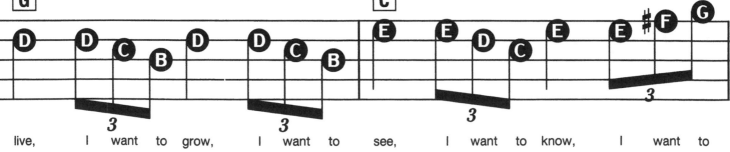

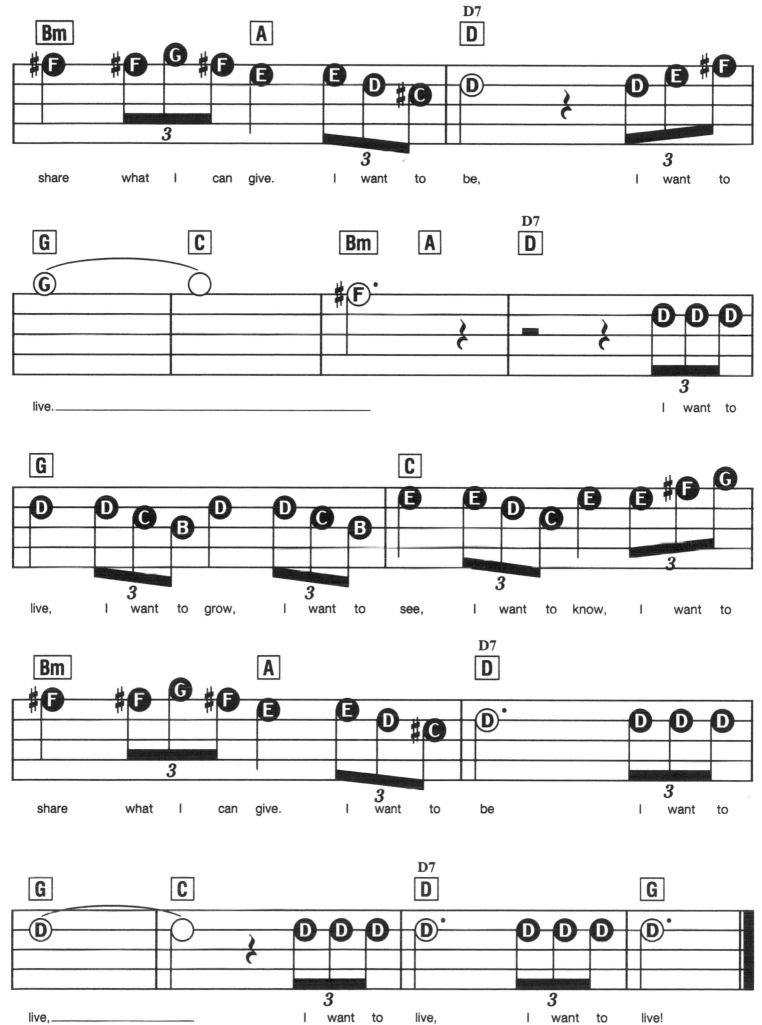

I'm Sorry

Registration 1
Rhythm: Fox Trot or Ballad

Words and Music by
John Denver

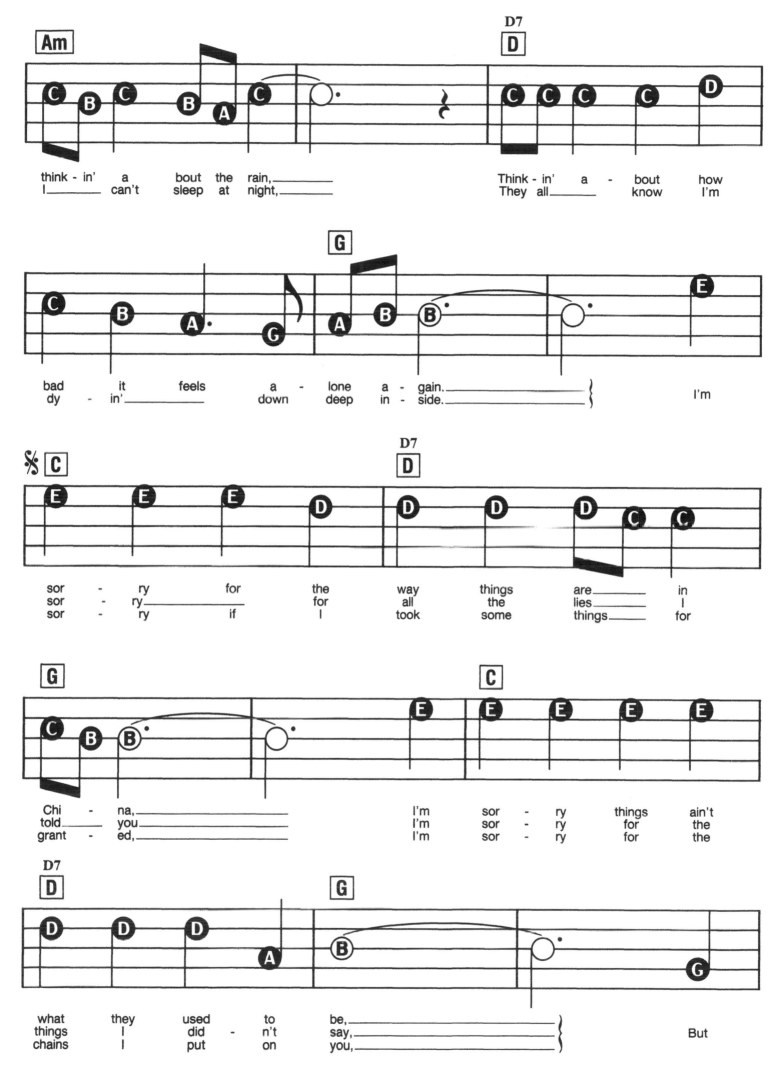

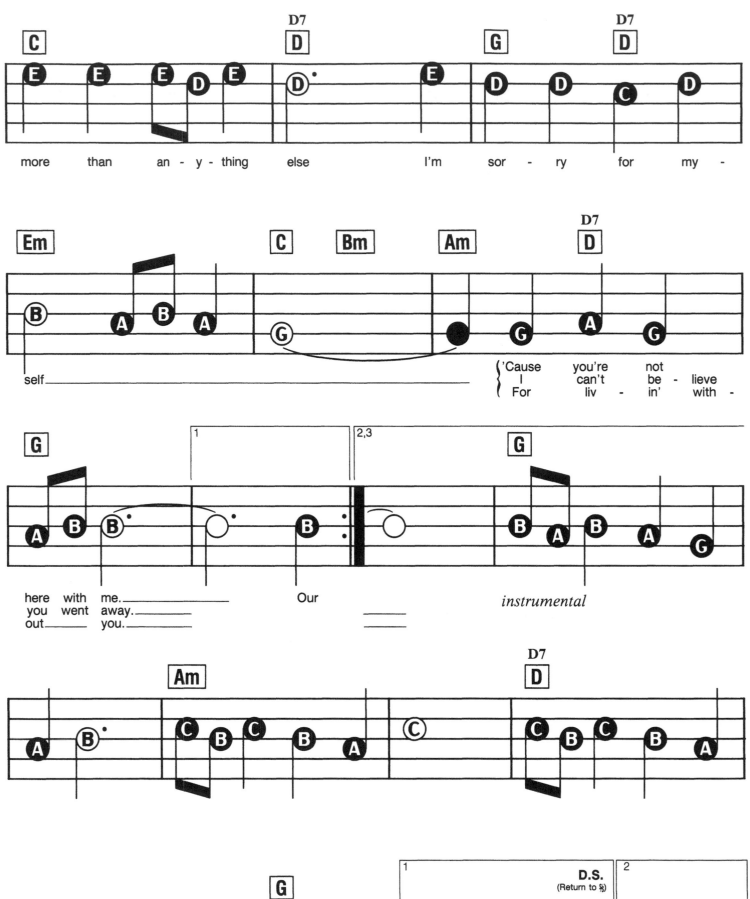

more than an - y - thing else ... I'm sor - ry for my -

self ...

'Cause you're not
I can't be - lieve
For liv - in' with -

here with me. ...
you went away. ...
out you. ...

Our

instrumental

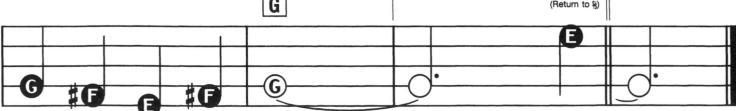

My Sweet Lady

Registration 2
Rhythm: Fox Trot or Ballad

Words and Music by
John Denver

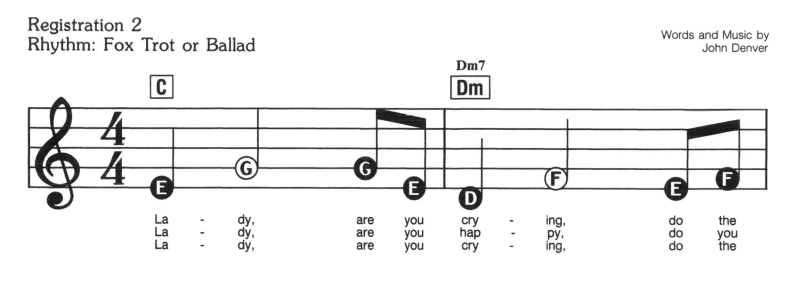

La - dy, are you cry - ing, do the
La - dy, are you hap - py, do you
La - dy, are you cry - ing, do the

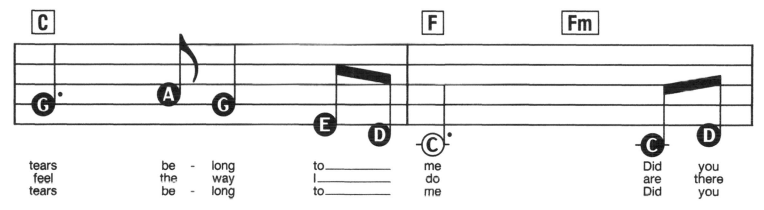

tears be - long to____ me Did you
feel the way I____ do are you
tears be - long to____ me Did you

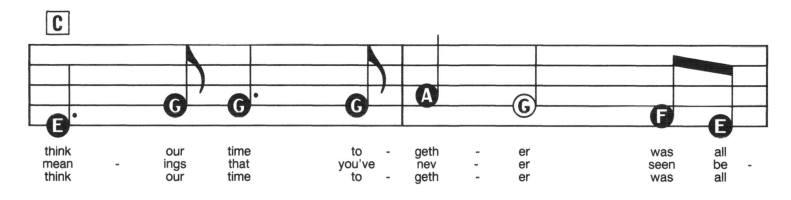

think our time to - geth - er was all
mean - ings that you've nev - er seen all be -
think our time to - geth - er was all

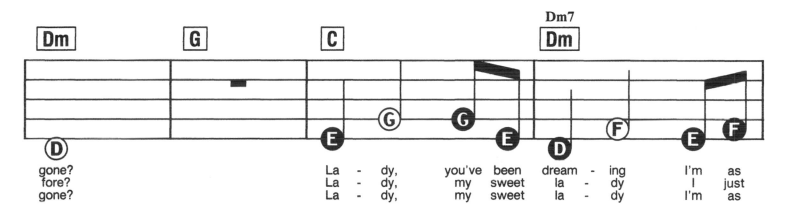

gone? La - dy, you've been dream - ing I'm as
fore? La - dy, my sweet la - dy I just
gone? La - dy, my sweet la - dy I'm as

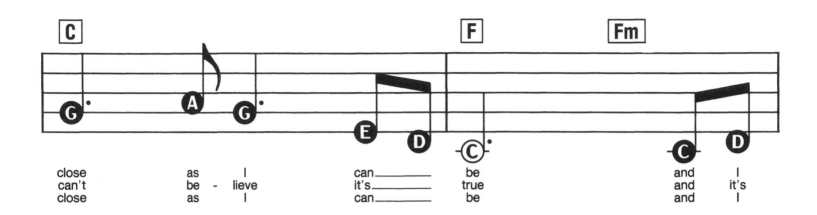

close ... as ... I ... can_____ ... be ... and ... I
can't ... be - lieve ... it's_____ ... true ... and ... it's
close ... as ... I ... can_____ ... be ... and ... I

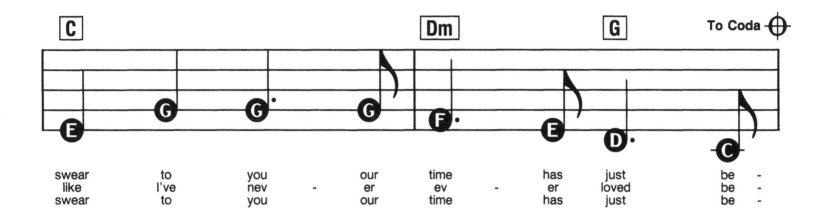

swear ... to ... you ... our ... time ... has ... just ... be -
like ... I've ... nev - er ... ev - er ... just ... loved ... be -
swear ... to ... you ... our ... time ... has ... just ... be -

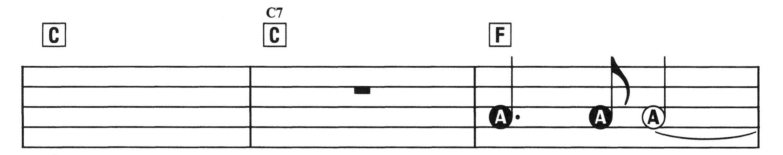

gun.
fore.

Close ... your ... eyes_____

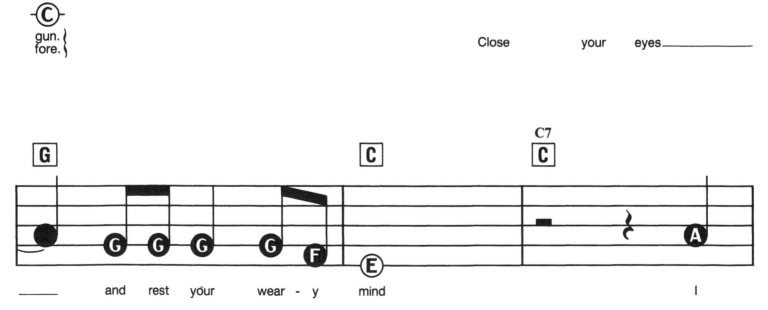

_____ ... and ... rest ... your ... wear - y ... mind ... I

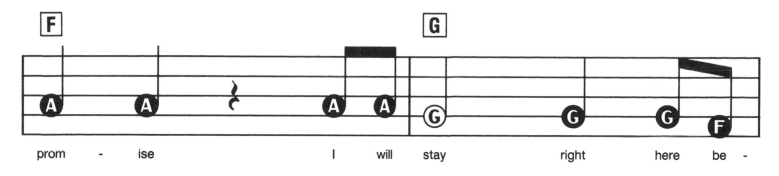

prom - ise   I will stay   right here be -

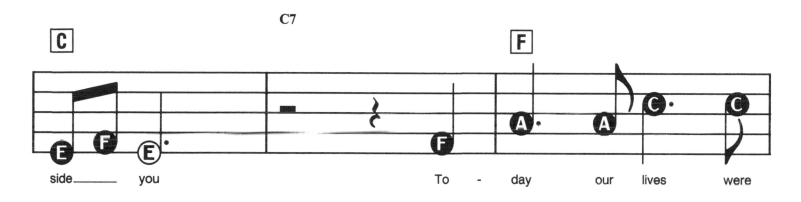

side____ you   To - day   our lives were

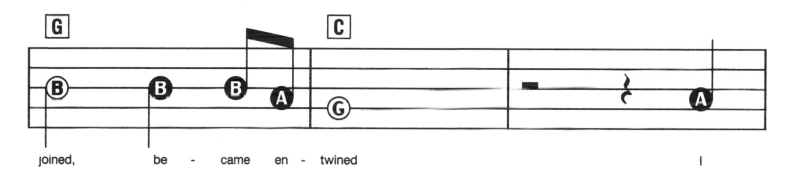

joined,   be - came en - twined   I

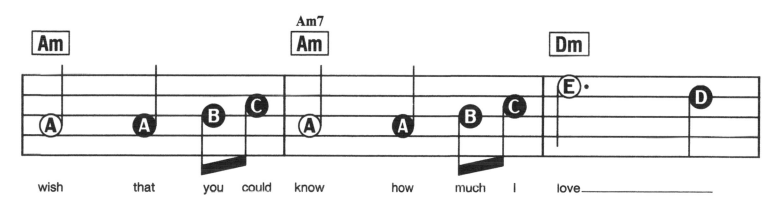

wish   that   you could   know   how much I   love____

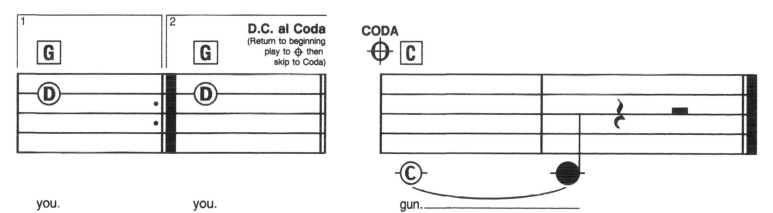

you.   you.   gun.____

Leaving On a Jet Plane

Registration 2
Rhythm: Fox Trot or Swing

Words and Music by
John Denver

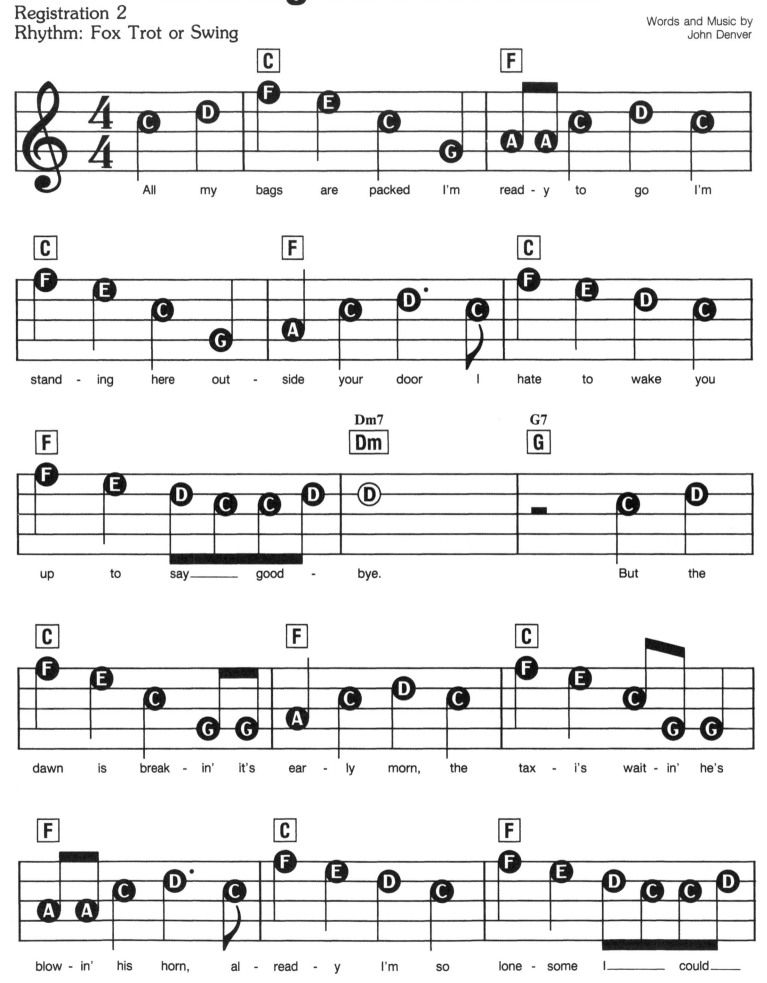

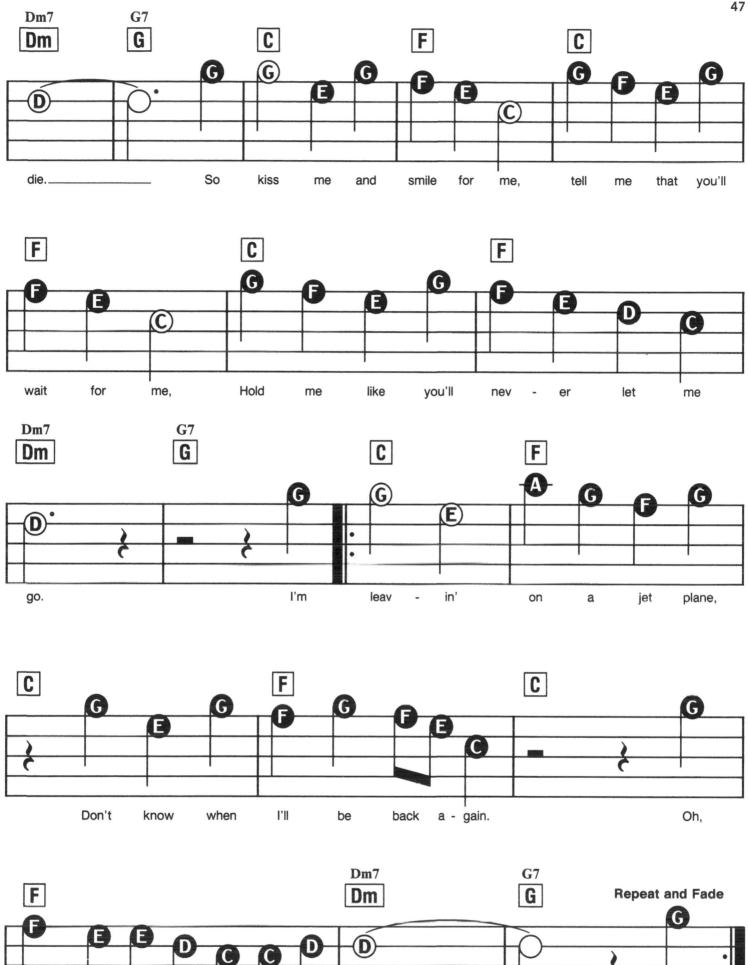

Like A Sad Song

Registration 5
Rhythm: Rock

Words and Music by
John Denver

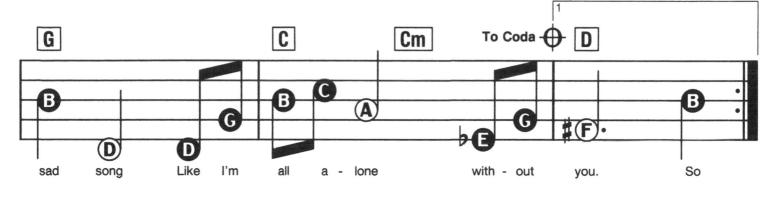

sad song Like I'm all a - lone with - out you. So

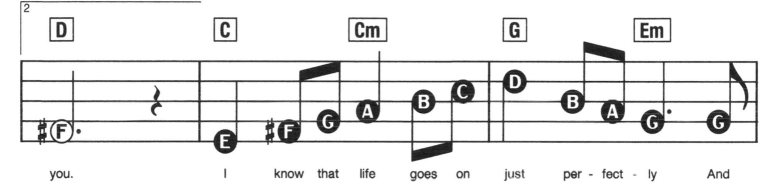

you. I know that life goes on just per - fect - ly And

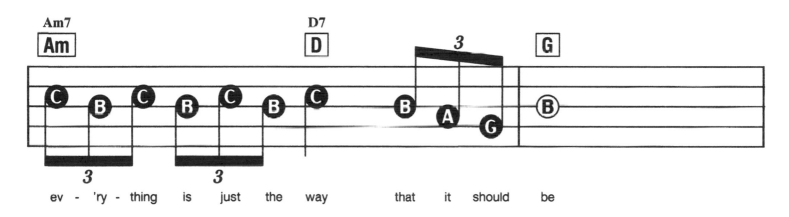

ev - 'ry - thing is just the way that it should be

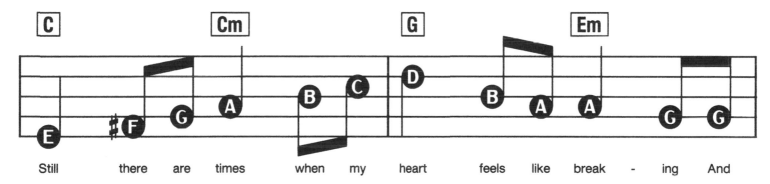

Still there are times when my heart feels like break - ing And

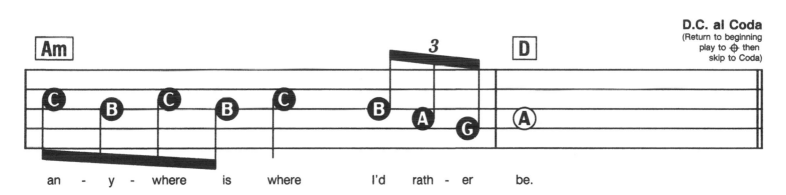

an - y - where is where I'd rath - er be.

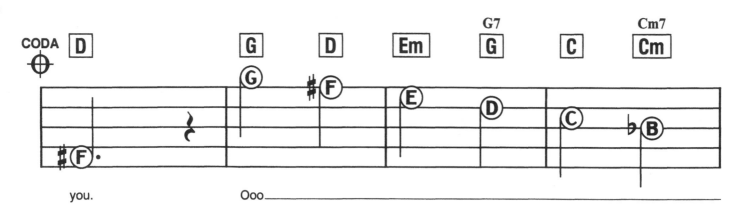

you. Ooo_____

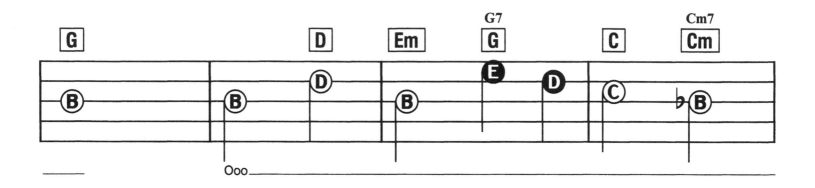

___ Ooo_____

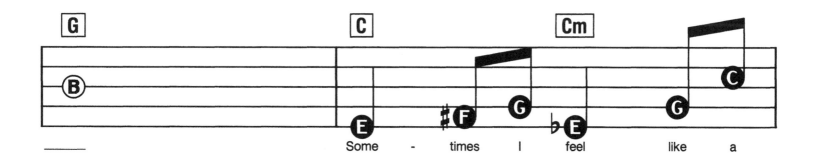

___ Some - times I feel like a

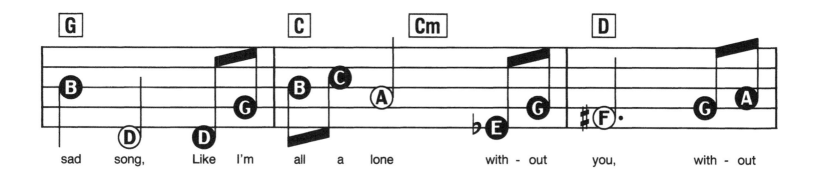

sad song, Like I'm all a lone with - out you, with - out

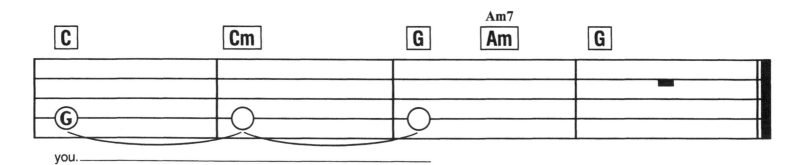

you._____

Rocky Mountain High

Registration 4
Rhythm: Country

Words and Music by
John Denver and Mike Taylor

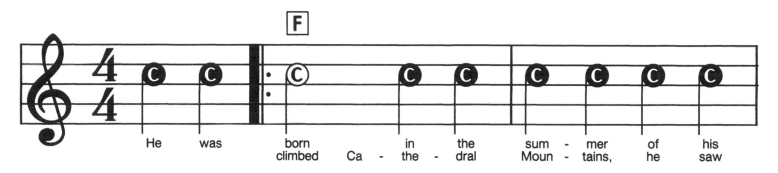

He was born in the sum - mer of his
climbed Ca - the - dral Moun - tains, he saw his

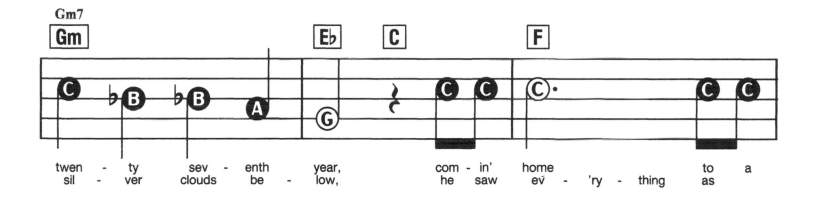

twen - ty sev - enth year, com - in' home to a
sil - ver clouds be - low, he saw ev́ - 'ry - thing as

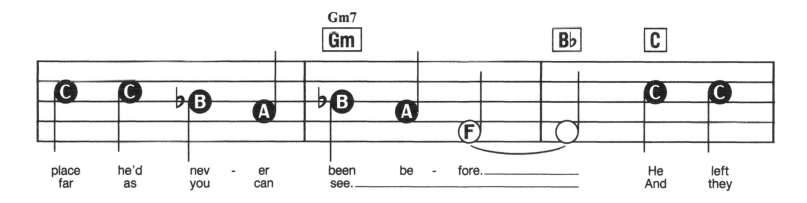

place he'd nev - er been be - fore. He left
far as you can see. And they

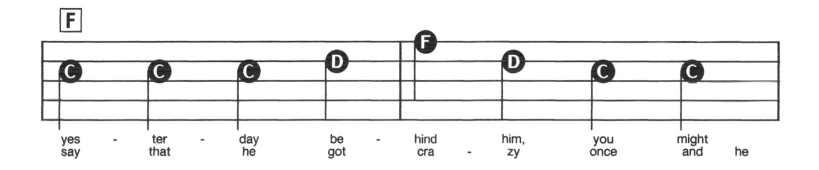

yes - ter - day be - hind him, you might
say that he got cra - zy once and he

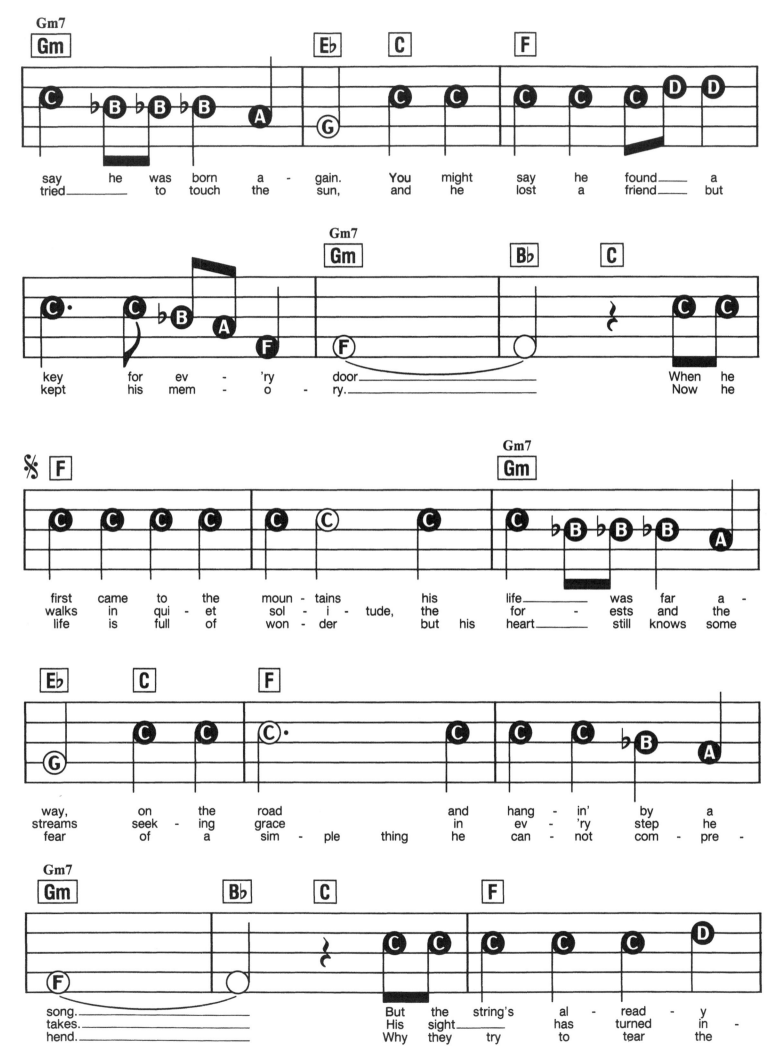

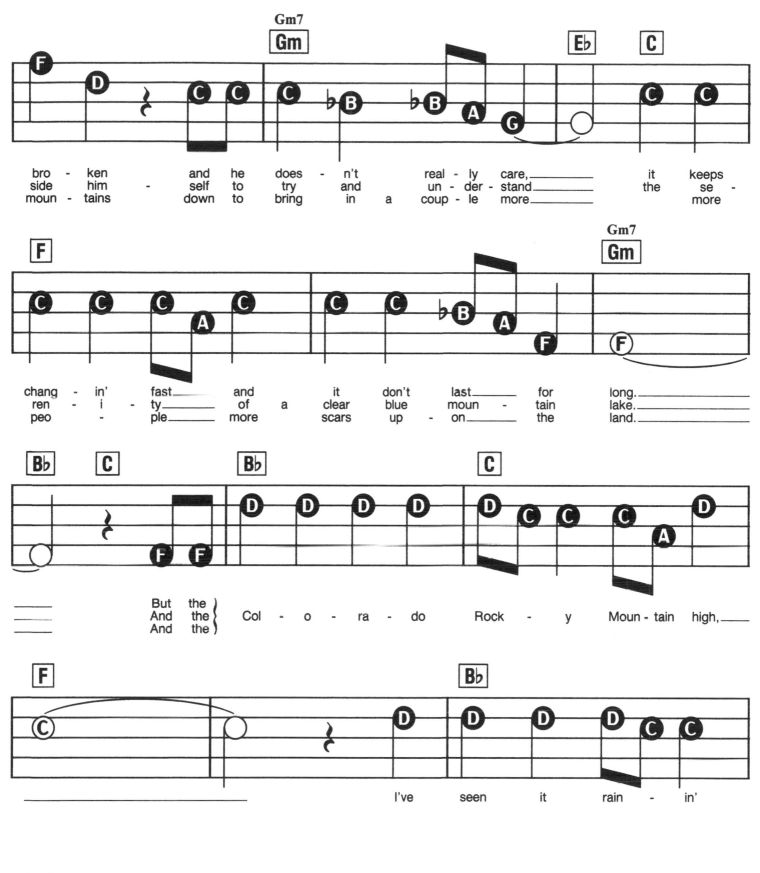

bro - ken — and he does - n't real - ly care,_____ it keeps
side him - self to try and un - der - stand_____ the se -
moun - tains down to bring in a coup - le more_____ more

chang - in' fast_____ and it don't last_____ for long._____
ren - i - ty_____ of a clear blue last moun - tain lake._____
peo - ple_____ more scars up - on_____ the land._____

_____ But the }
_____ And the } Col - o - ra - do Rock - y Moun - tain high,_____
_____ And the }

I've seen it rain - in'

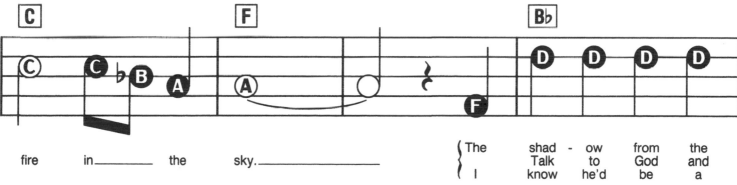

fire in_____ the sky._____

{ The shad - ow from the
Talk to God and
{ I know he'd be a

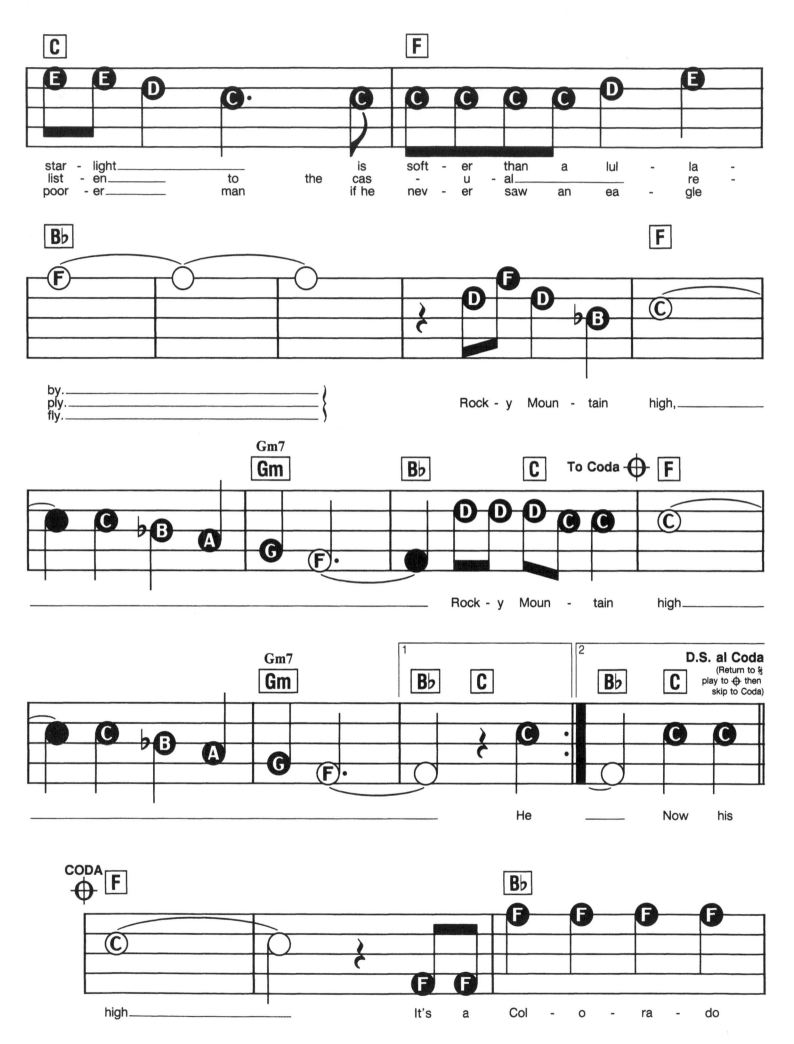

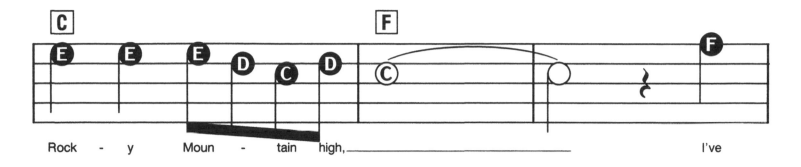

Rock - y Moun - tain high,_____ I've

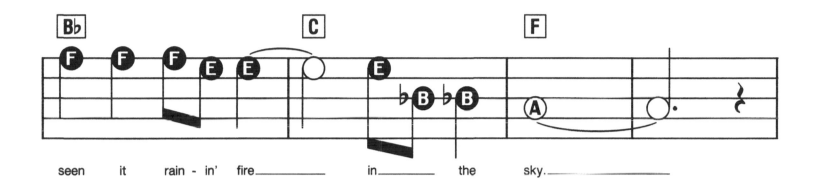

seen it rain - in' fire_____ in_____ the sky._____

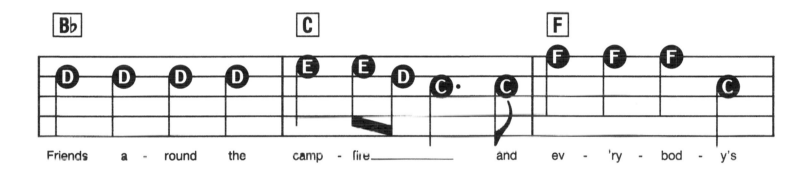

Friends a - round the camp - fire_____ and ev - 'ry - bod - y's

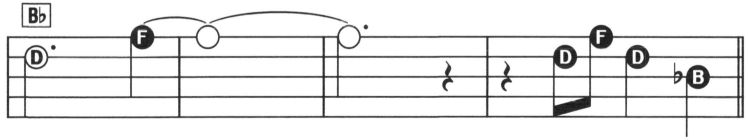

high._____ Rock - y Moun - tain

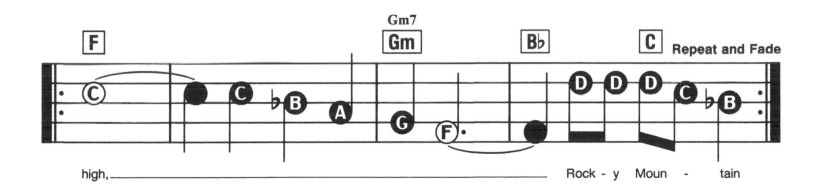

high,_____ Rock - y Moun - tain

Looking For Space

Registration 1
Rhythm: Fox Trot or Ballad

Words and Music by
John Denver

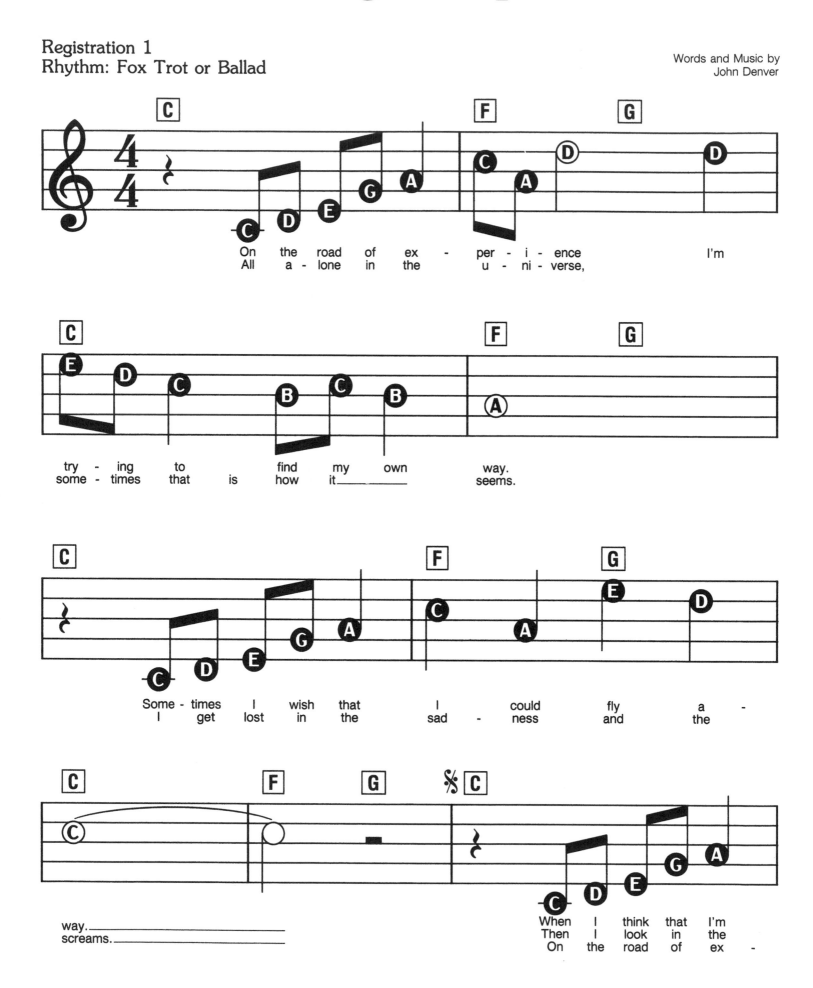

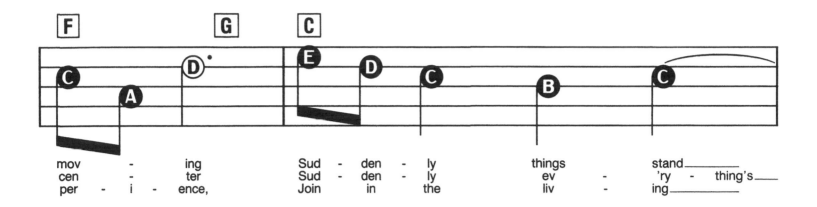

mov - ing | Sud - den - ly | things stand_____
cen - ter | Sud - den - ly | ev - 'ry - thing's_____
per - i - ence, | Join in the | liv - ing_____

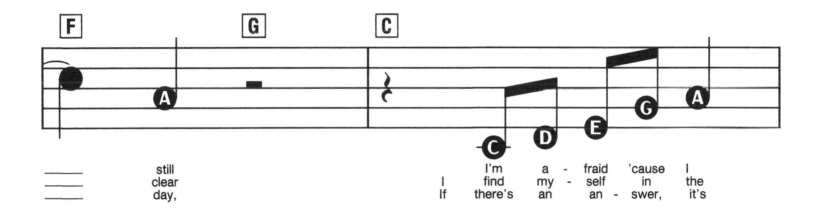

_____ still | I'm a - fraid 'cause I
_____ clear | If there's an an - swer, it's
_____ day, |

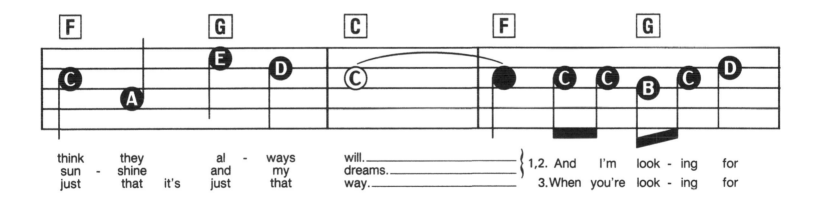

think they al - ways | will._____ | 1,2. And I'm look - ing for
sun - shine and my | dreams._____ | 3. When you're look - ing for
just that it's just that | way._____ |

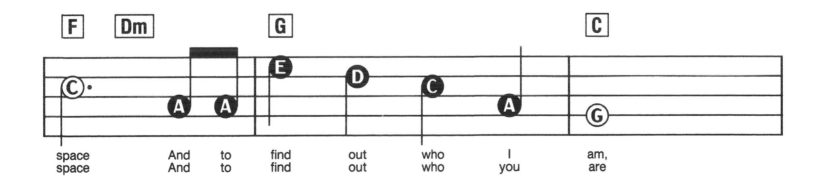

space | And to | find out who I am,
space | And to | find out who you are

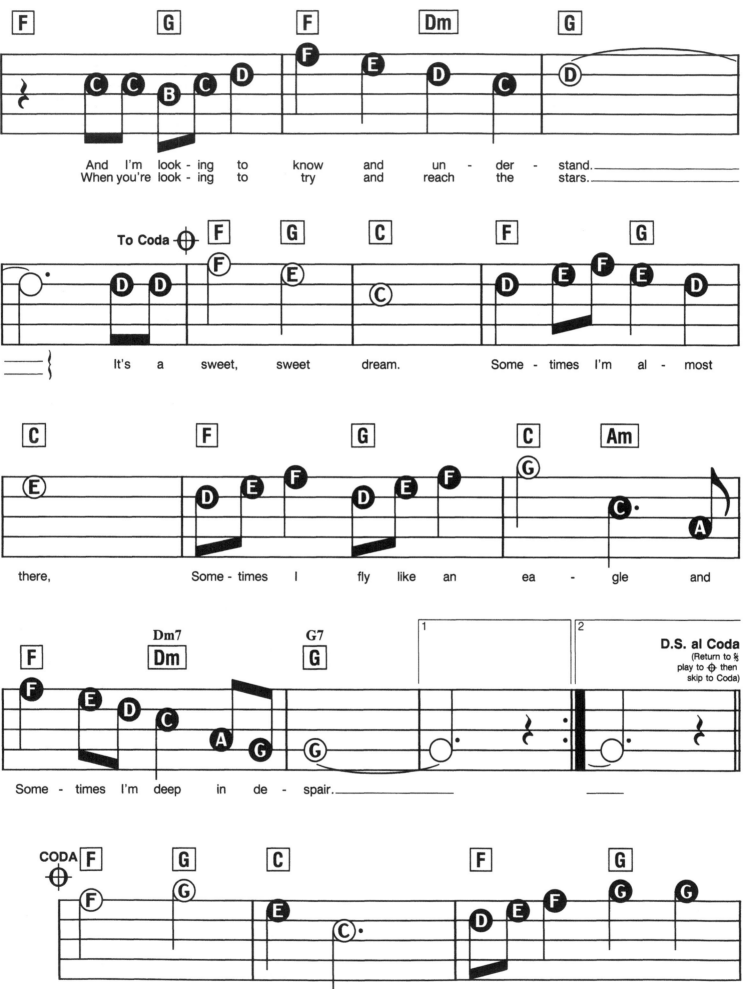

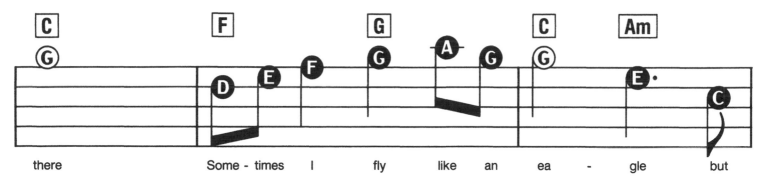

there · Some - times I fly like an ea - gle but

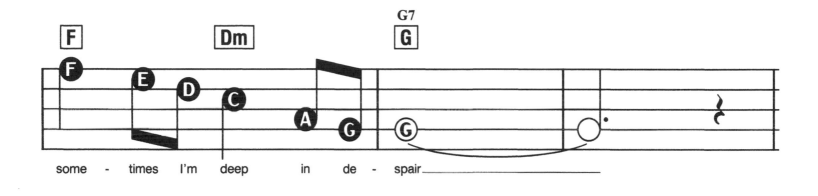

some - times I'm deep in de - spair

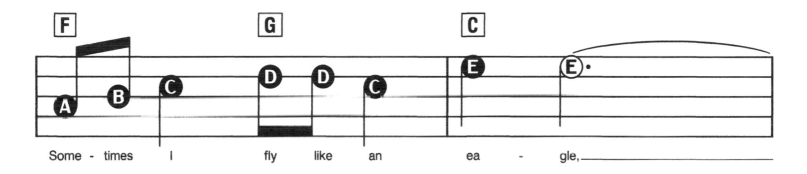

Some - times I fly like an ea - gle,

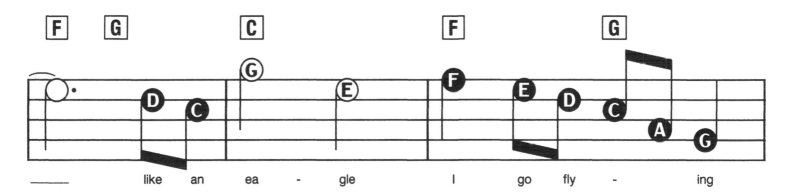

like an ea - gle I go fly - ing

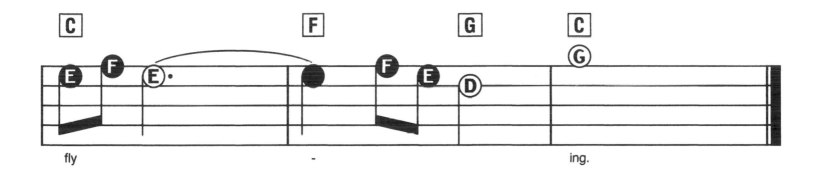

fly - ing.

Perhaps Love

Registration 1
Rhythm: Fox Trot or Ballad

Words and Music by
John Denver

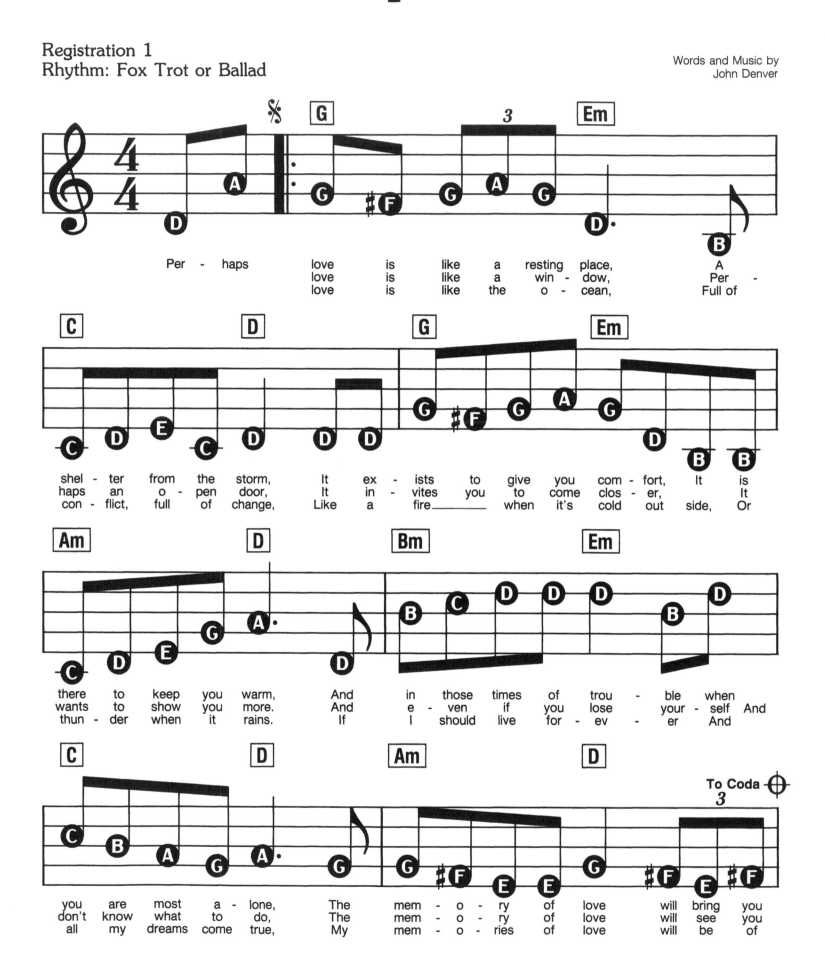

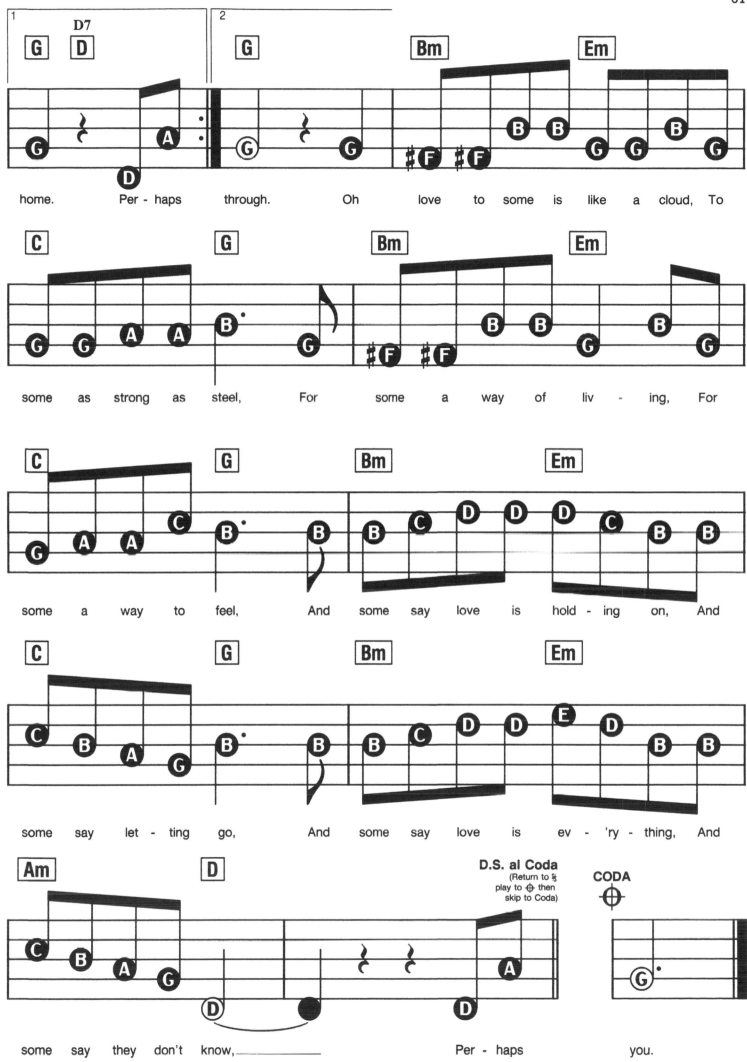

Poems, Prayers And Promises

Registration 4
Rhythm: Country

Words and Music by
John Denver

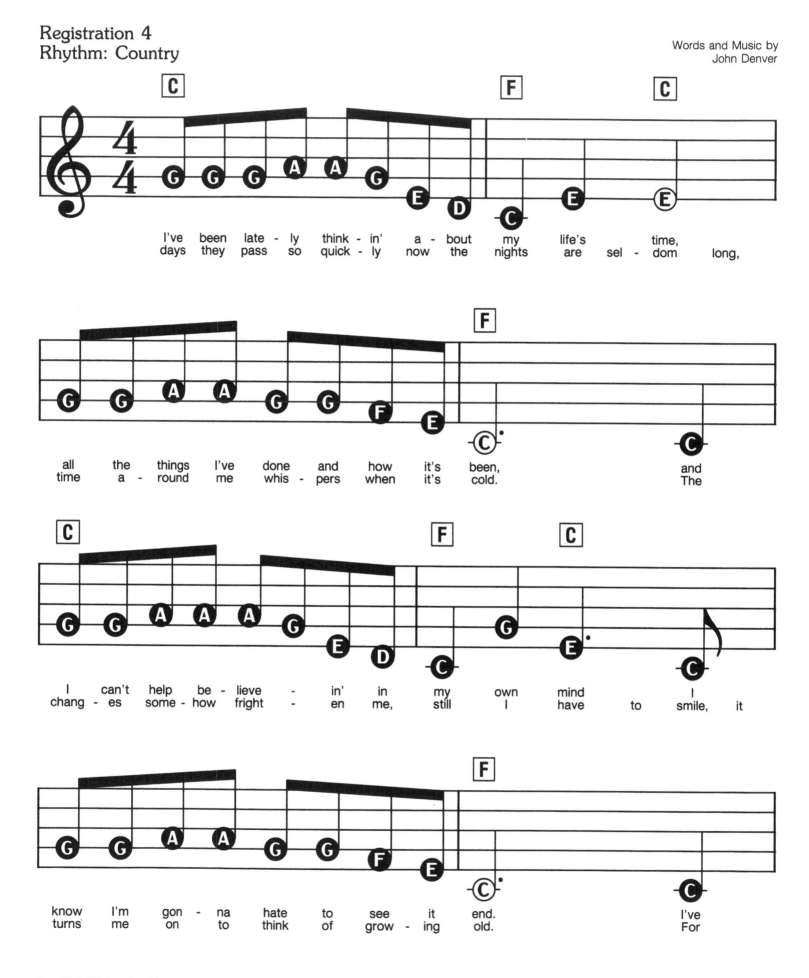

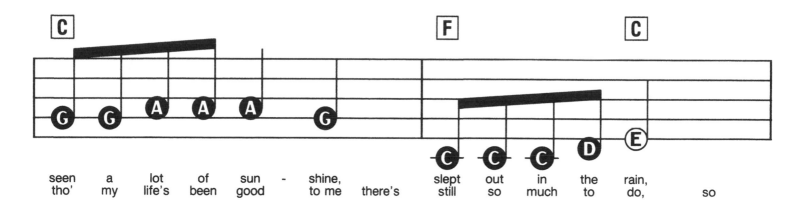

seen a lot of sun - shine,
tho' my life's been good, to me there's

slept out in the rain,
still so much to do, so

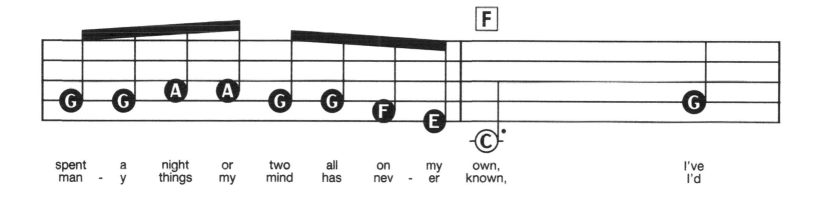

spent a night or two all on my own,
man - y things my mind has nev - er known,

I've
I'd

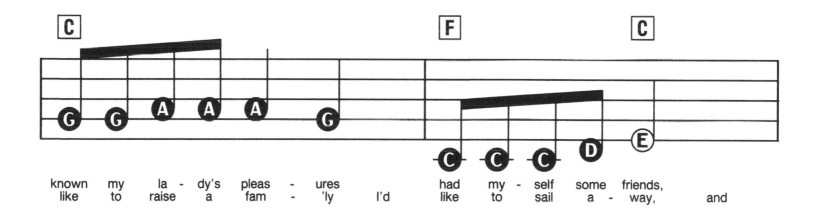

known my la - dy's pleas - ures
like to raise a fam - 'ly I'd

had my - self some friends,
like to sail a - way, and

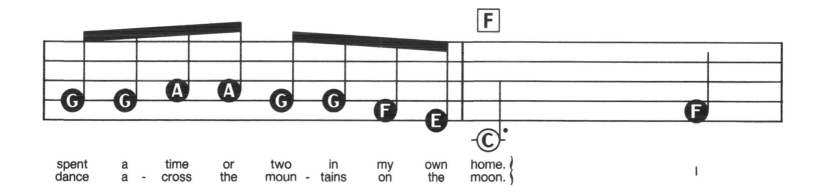

spent a time or two in my own home.
dance a - cross the moun - tains on the moon.

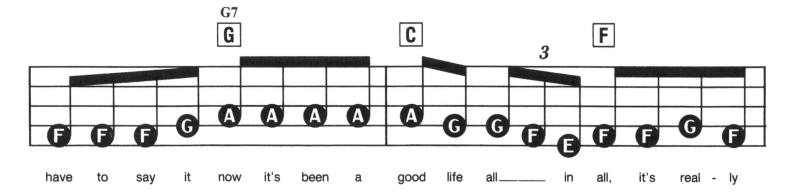

have to say it now it's been a good life all_____ in all, it's real - ly

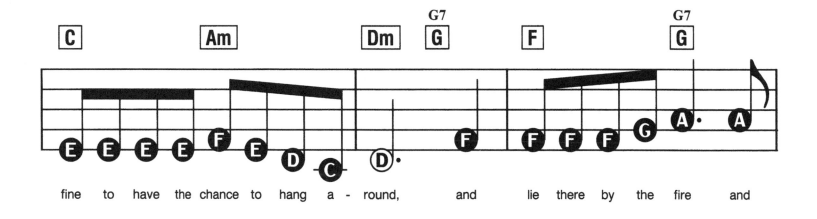

fine to have the chance to hang a - round, and lie there by the fire and

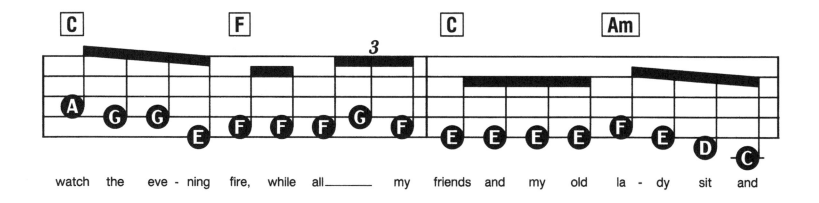

watch the eve - ning fire, while all_____ my friends and my old la - dy sit and

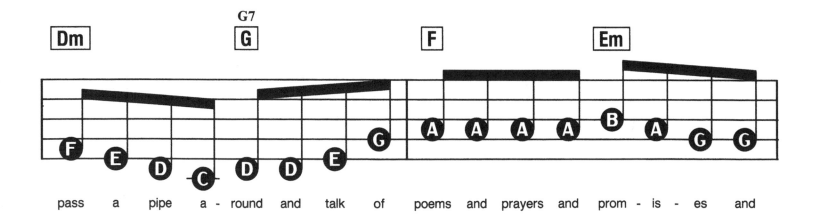

pass a pipe a - round and talk of poems and prayers and prom - is - es and

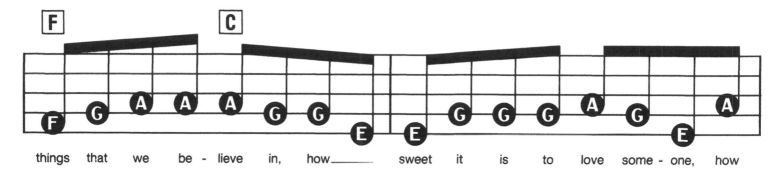

things that we be - lieve in, how_____ sweet it is to love some - one, how

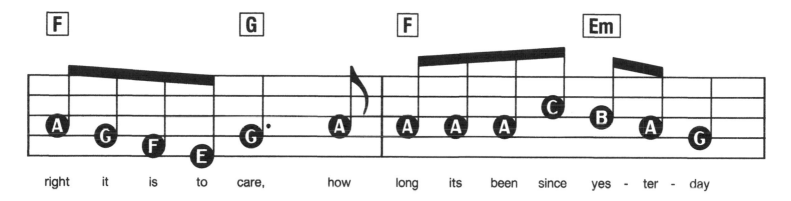

right it is to care, how long its been since yes - ter - day

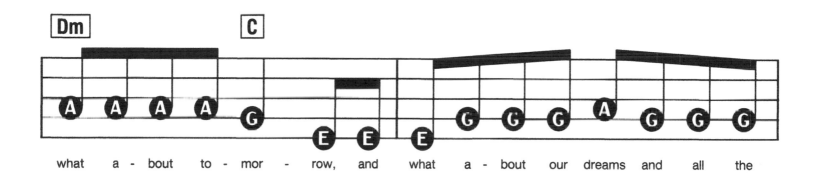

what a - bout to - mor - row, and what a - bout our dreams and all the

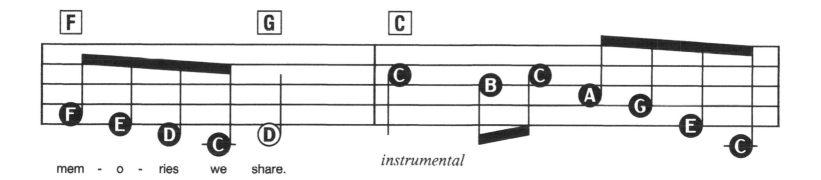

mem - o - ries we share. *instrumental*

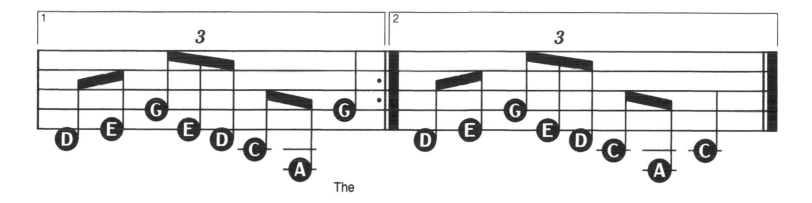

The

Rhymes And Reasons

Registration 10
Rhythm: Country

Words and Music by
John Denver

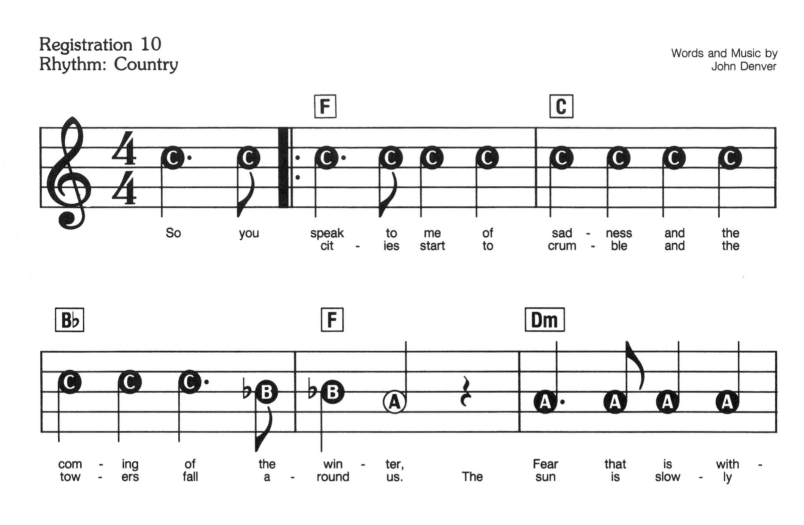

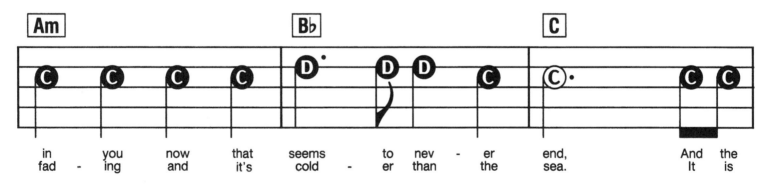

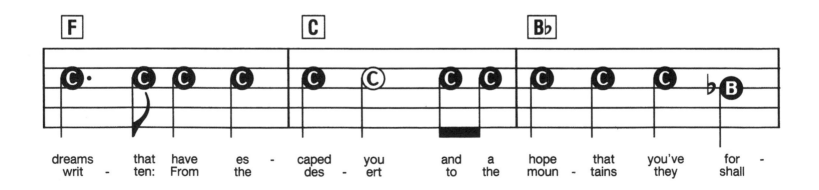

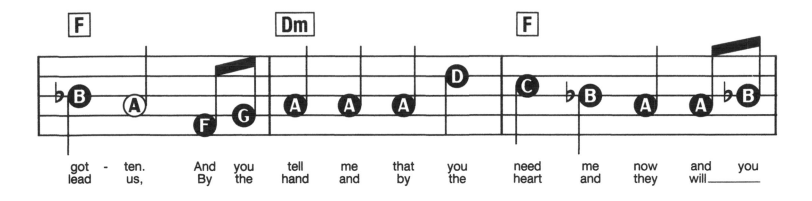

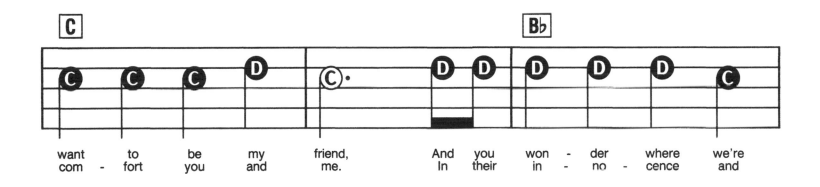

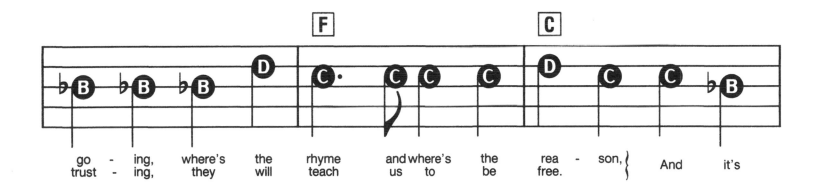

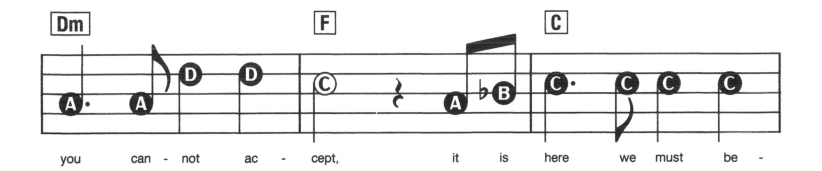

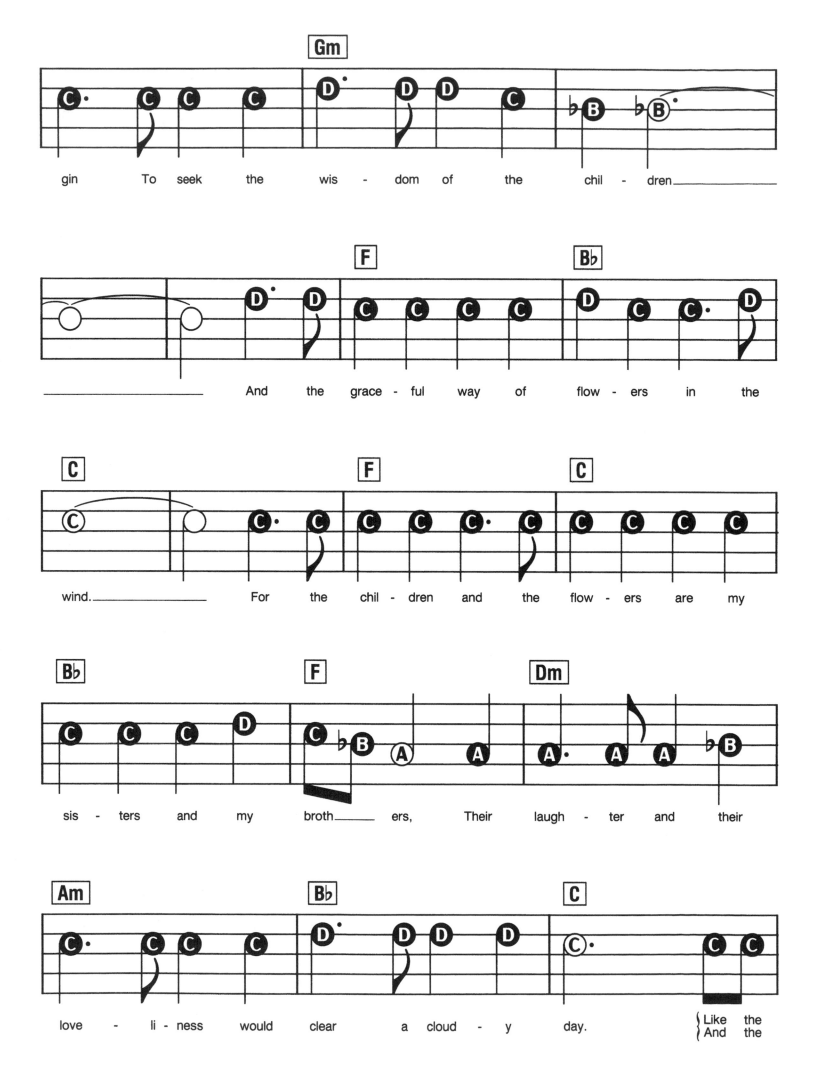

69

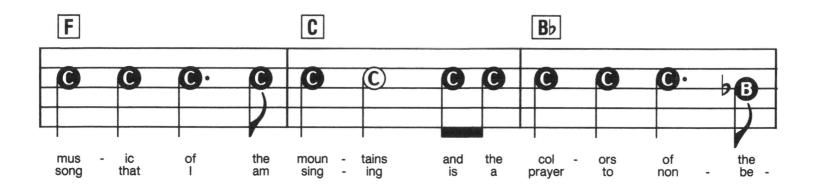

mus - ic of the moun - tains and the col - ors of the
song that I am sing - ing is a prayer to non - be -

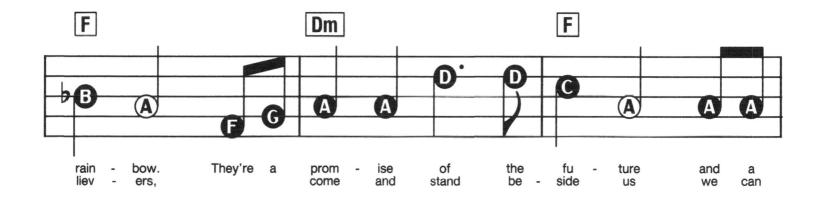

rain - bow. They're a prom - ise of the fu - ture and a
liev - ers, come and stand be - side us and we can

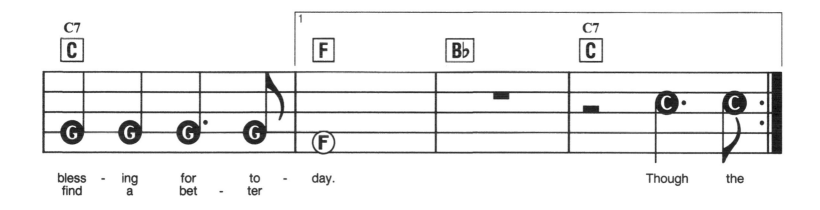

bless - ing for to - day. Though the
find a bet - ter

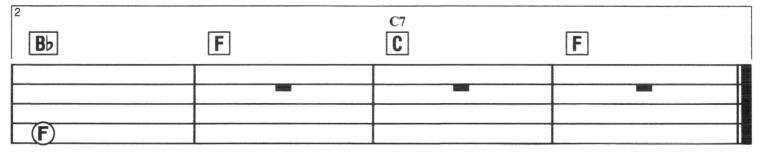

way.

Some Days Are Diamonds
(Some Days Are Stone)

Registration 7
Rhythm: Soft Rock

Words and Music by
Dick Feller

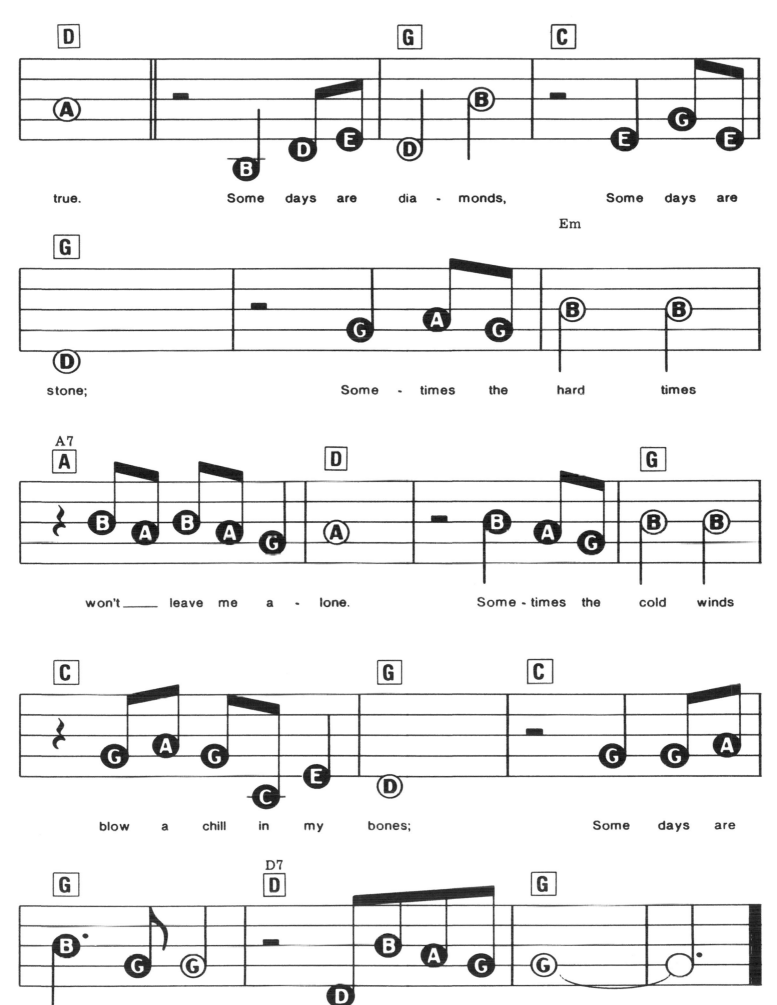

Sunshine On My Shoulders

Words by John Denver
Music by John Denver, Mike Taylor
and Dick Kniss

Registration 1
Rhythm: Fox Trot or Ballad

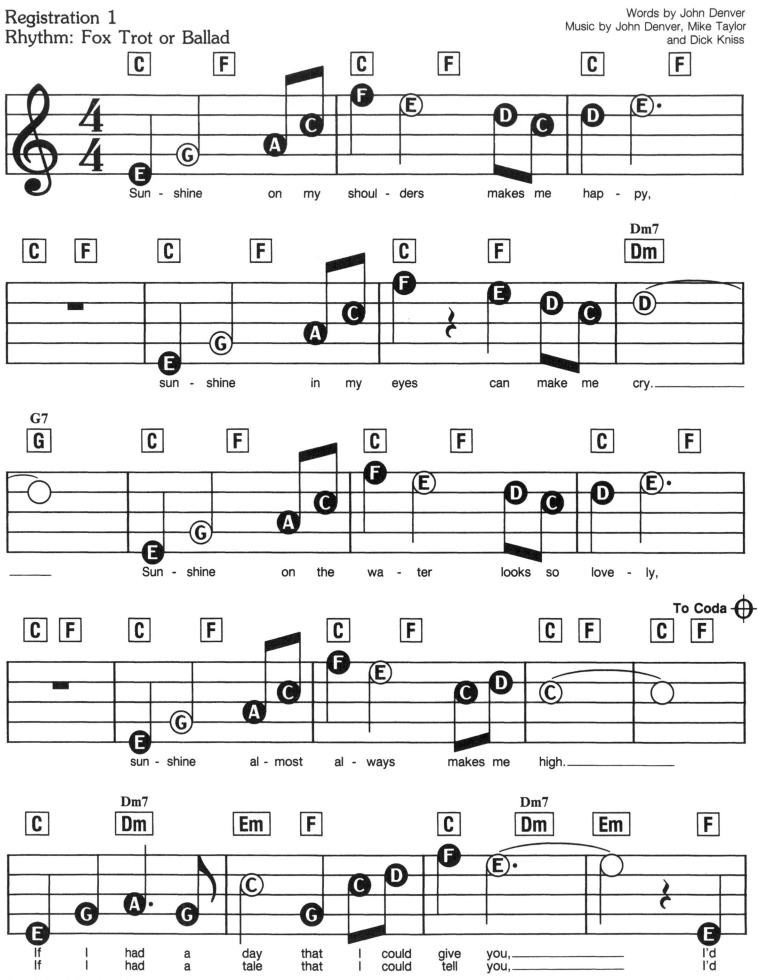

73

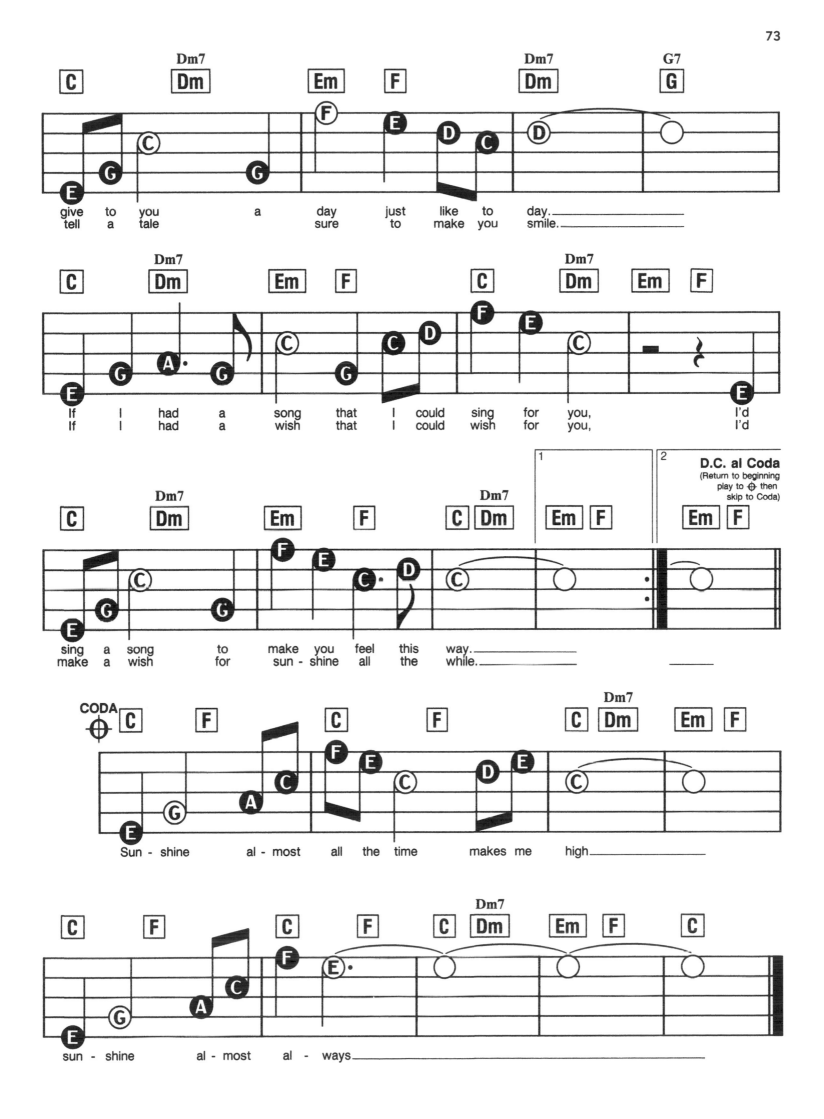

Take Me Home, Country Roads

Registration 10
Rhythm: Country

Words and Music by Bill Danoff,
Taffy Nivert and John Denver

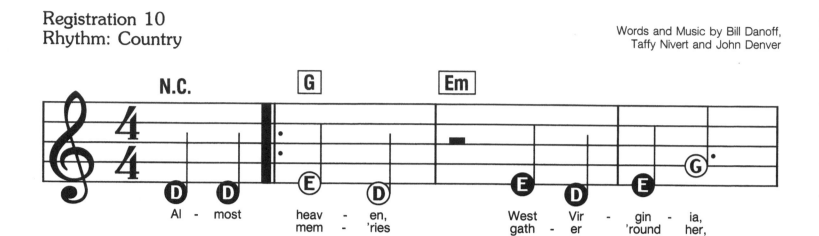

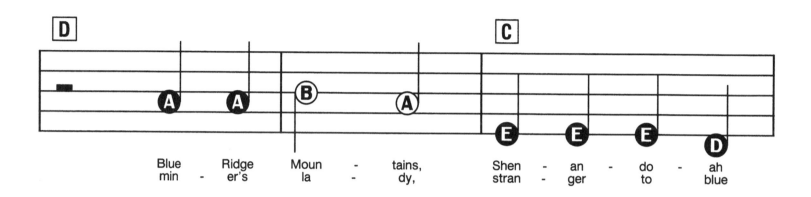

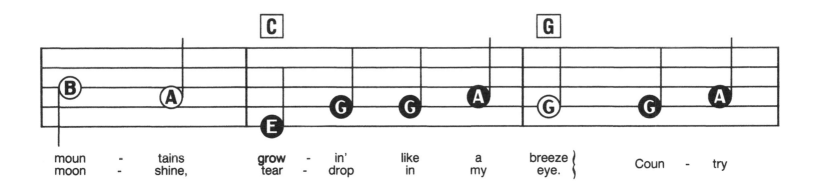

moun - tains grow - in' like a breeze
moon - shine, tear - drop in my eye. } Coun - try

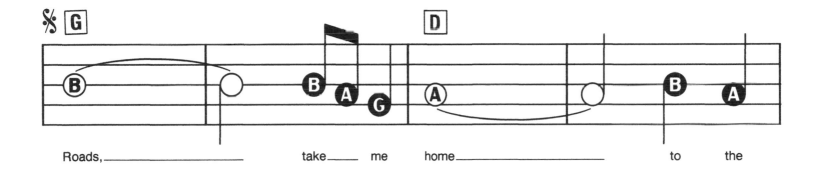

Roads,_____ take___ me home_____ to the

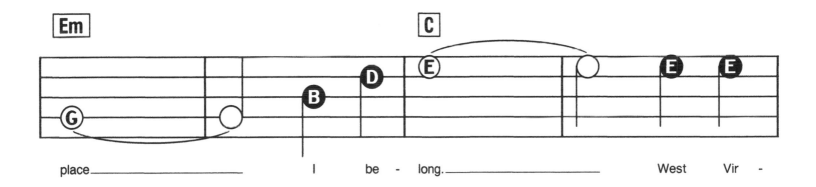

place_____ I be - long._____ West Vir -

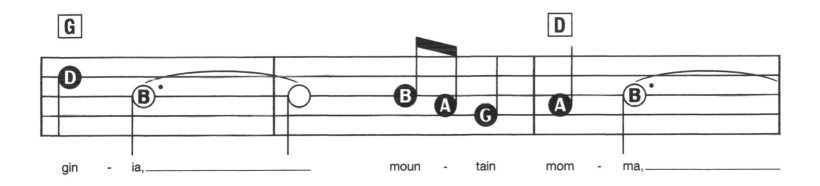

gin - ia,_____ moun - tain mom - ma,_____

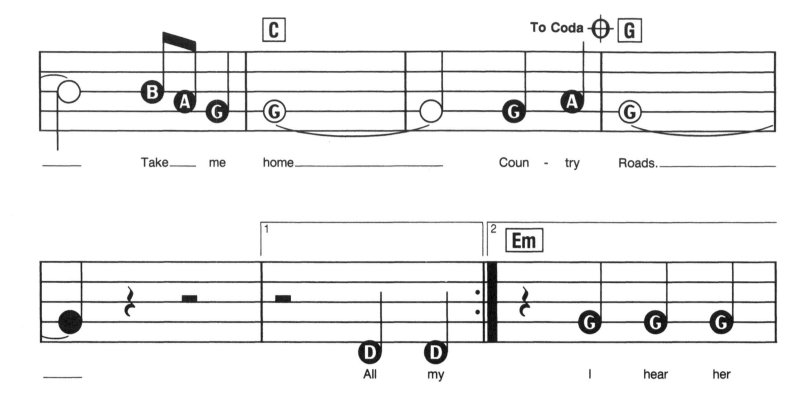

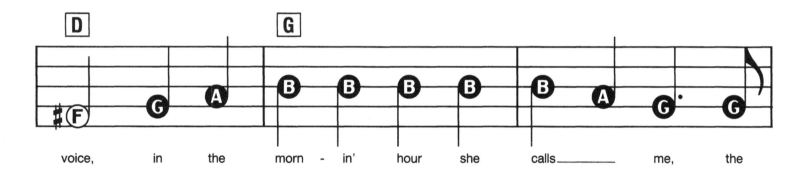

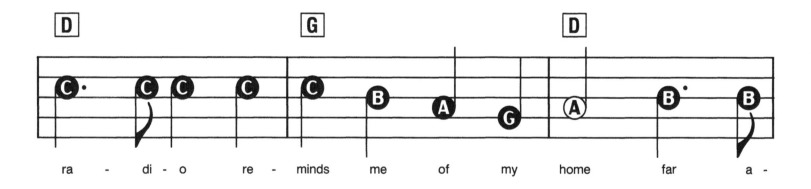

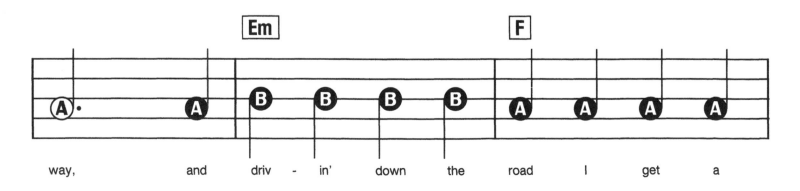

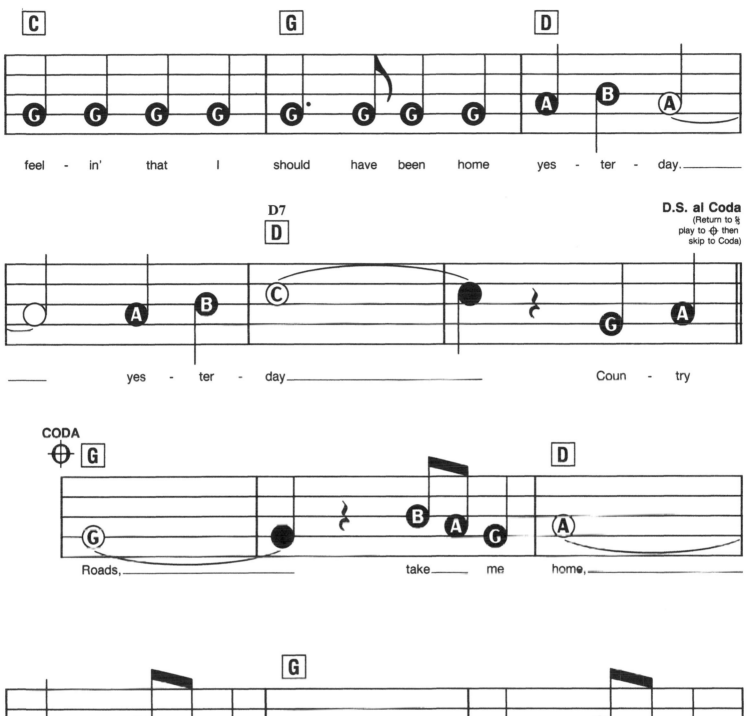

feel - in' that I should have been home yes - ter - day.

yes - ter - day Coun - try

CODA

Roads, take me home,

Coun - try Roads, take me

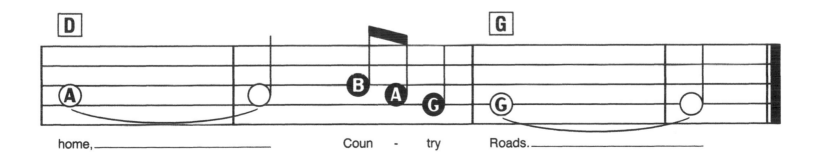

home, Coun - try Roads.

Thank God I'm A Country Boy

Registration 10
Rhythm: Country

Words and Music by
John Martin Sommers

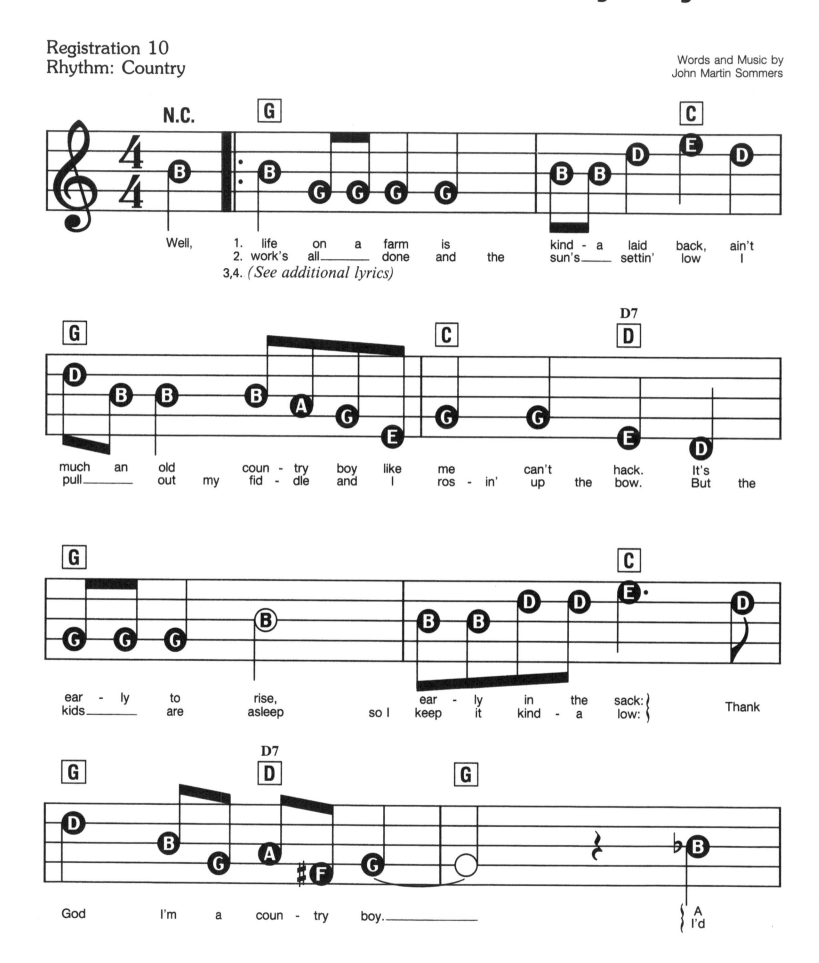

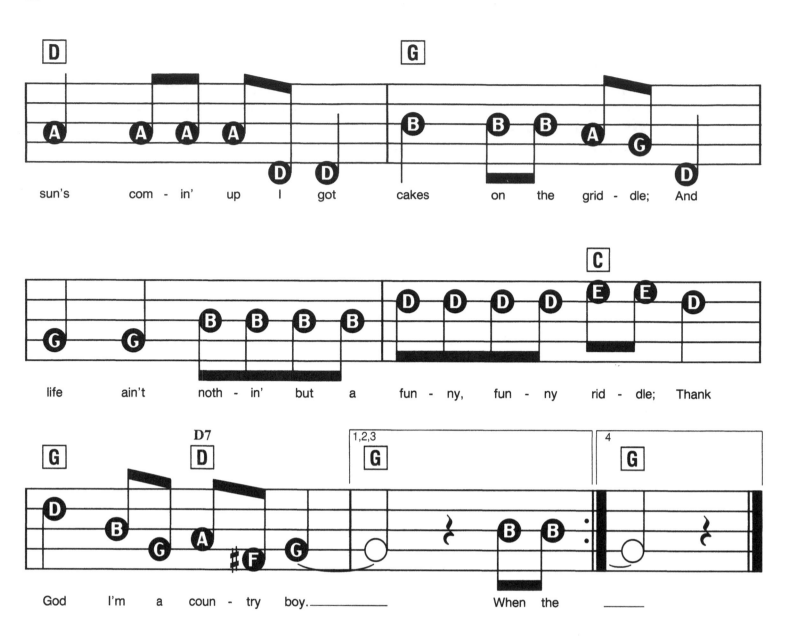

sun's com - in' up I got cakes on the grid - dle; And

life ain't noth - in' but a fun - ny, fun - ny rid - dle; Thank

God I'm a coun - try boy. When the

Additional Lyrics

Verse 3
I wouldn't trade my life for diamonds or jewels,
I never was one of them money hungry fools.
I'd rather have my fiddle and my farmin' tools:
Thank God I'm a country boy.
Yeah, city folk drivin' in a black limousine,
A lotta sad people thinkin' that's mighty keen.
Well, folks let me tell you now exactly what I mean:
I thank God I'm a country boy.

Verse 4
Well, my fiddle was my daddy's till the day he died,
And he took me by the hand and held me close to his side.
He said, "Live a good life and play my fiddle with pride,
And thank God you're a country boy."
My daddy taught me young how to hunt and how to whittle,
He taught me how to work and play a tune on the fiddle.
He taught me how to love and how to give just a little:
Thank God I'm a country boy.